speaking of
Curing
Diseases
through Yoga

GANESH JI

The Bestower of Peace, Happiness, Prosperity and Success

speaking of Curing Diseases through Yoga

Swami Durganand Saraswati
Swarga Ashram, Rishikesh,
Uttrakhand, The Himalayas

Sterling Paperbacks

STERLING PAPERBACKS
An imprint of
Sterling Publishers (P) Ltd.
A-59, Okhla Industrial Area, Phase-II,
New Delhi-110020.
Tel: 26387070, 26386209; Fax: 91-11-26383788
E-mail: mail@sterlingpublishers.com
www.sterlingpublishers.com

Speaking of Curing Diseases through Yoga
© 2011, Swami Durganand Saraswati
ISBN 978 81 207 6377 7

All rights are reserved.
No part of this publication may be reproduced, stored in a retrieval system or transmitted, in any form or by any means, mechanical, photocopying, recording or otherwise, without prior written permission of the author.

Printed in India

Printed and Published by Sterling Publishers Pvt. Ltd.,
New Delhi-110020.

Contents

	Preface	9
1.	History of Yogasanas	13
2.	Asanas Helpful in Digestion	20
3.	Leg Troubles	23
4.	Lack of Confidence	25
5.	Loss of Spirit	27
6.	Night Pollution	29
7.	Fearfulness	33
8.	Headache and Related Problems	36
9.	Hernia	40
10.	Wind in the Stomach (Tympanitis)	42
11.	Navel Displacement	44
12.	Sensual Thoughts	48
13.	Improvement of IQ	51
14.	Improving Concentration	53
15.	Prophet Mohammad Yoga	57
16.	Problem of Early Rising	61
17.	Deformities of Testicles or Related Problems	63
18.	Senility	65
19.	Dizziness	68
20.	Chronic Constipation	71
21.	Sciatica	74

22.	Backache	77
23.	Health Care System	79
24.	Knee Joint Problems	84
25.	Body Pain	86
26.	Stomach Problems	88
27.	Development of Personality	91
28.	Lung Diseases	95
29.	Diabetes	101
30.	Piles	106
31.	Blood Pressure	109
32.	Menstrual Problems	114
33.	Pot Belly	116
34.	Easy and Painless Delivery	118
35.	Dyspepsia or Indigestion	122
36.	Loss of Strength in the Arms	125
37.	Semen Preservation	127
38.	Skin Diseases	129
39.	Heavy Posterior	133
40.	Increase Your height	135
41.	Spleen Disease	137
42.	Maha Mudra	141
43.	Asana for General Health and Well-being	143
44.	Loss of Appetite	145
45.	Pain in the Neck	150
46.	Fidgeting	153
47.	Nervousness	156
48.	Sleeplessness (Insomnia)	158
49.	Liver Diseases	162
50.	Ear Complaints	170

Contents

51.	Breathing Exercises or Pranayama	172
52.	Dental Health	176
53.	Liberation or Salvation	179
54.	Yogasanas Further Discussed	187
55.	Nauli	192
56.	Some other Problems	193

*Of those
who remain absorbed
in the absorption of the Absolute
Almighty many-many times in the caves
of the Himalayas, of those whose heart is hurt
and moved at the distress of the real aspirants
and of those who render most useful
services to the humanity,
Swami Durganand Saraswati
is one so far as my personal experience
goes. This books is sure to
render yeoman's
services both to the
aspirants and patients.*

Dr. David Wells, USA
*Veteran Yoga Teacher
and Ayurvedic Doctor*

Preface

By the grace of the Almighty, like the words Dharam Karam in India, Yoga is also now a household name especially in the Western countries. Therefore, the number of books on yoga is increasing day by day. After going through some books, I thought it to be needful to disperse the blessings of Yoga, especially in respect of curing diseases to the pupils who are sincerely eager to turn over a new leaf by adopting a full-fledged yogic way of life, or who are unluckily suffering from various kinds of diseases because of which they live a stressful life and waste thousands of money but of no avail or of a temporary consolation only.

The yoga of asanas is the most scientific variety of ontology ever deciphered till this day under the Sun. There is no system which can challenge the hygienic validity in so shortest a time as Yoga is capable of. We should worship the foot-dust of the lotus feet of the Seer sages by whose magnanimous benedictions we can try to practise yoga today.

Yoga of asanas and pranayamas (breathing exercises) are as old as the Sun God. The historians are not unanimous in their opinions as to the oldness of this spiritual knowledge. Countless manuscripts have been destroyed by jealous, narrow-minded, communal and base-born torturous kings; another wave of worldly play had started; again destroyed and again another destruction. This has been the play for a long time out of memory.

To come to the subject, the bone of contention of the world of hygiene which is connected with Yoga of physiological exercises, is diet or food. Diet is a substituting theological or philosophical

Speaking of Curing Diseases through Yoga

word for food on the ground that Sages looked upon human beings as great sufferers of misery – a cancerous disease and, hence, they use this word 'diet'. A most sorry state of affairs of the day is that there is no or hardly any food or drink which is perfectly healthful except water of some places – a fact which is known to Naturopaths than any man in the street.

There are at least two reasons which count for such a pathetic state: One is overpopulation and the other is misguiding guidance or commerciality. The rise in population being out of hands of the government of many countries, the production is needed to boost up in order to feed the extra mouths every year. It is impossible to produce more food in a natural way since the soil capacity decreases every year. So, under the compulsion of circumstances, inorganic food stuff has made an unrestricted access into the world markets. The result being that a lay man is absolutely unaware of the real nature, character or taste of the real food.

Edibles, thanks to the research of food technologists, look apparently attractive but produce a highly incurable effect on the human economy. Nowadays cows are being injected to become fat for procuring more meat; the result of such an absolutely unintelligent policy has given birth to epidemic diseases among cows leading to a loss of money, perhaps, millions. Readers may have become aware of this fact through newspapers. Adulteration is no more a secret nowadays. It is no matter of the day. The fruits that are sold in most markets of the world are ripened artificially by using a heavy amount of toxic chemicals, especially carbide gas which is used to burn lamps. Injurious insecticides are spread on them against premature damage. So is the case of vegetables.

Cow's milk, the most balanced food, is highly injurious in most cases; first of all, the milk is produced artificially for, cow is served with the food that is highly chemical. Cows live hardly on green grass – the food that should be given to them. It is, perhaps

Preface

known to many readers that green grass has been in use by a number of Yogins among whom the name of Durbasaji is well known. Durba or Doorba means green grass. According to media reports, milk is now being manufactured from even animal skin, potato, etc. Such is the state of the food product. According to *Srimad Bhagvad Gita,* "Man is what he eats". One day I prepared some aubergines but could not eat them on account of its excessive bitterness. I tried giving it to the cow but it also refused to eat it.

However, diseases can be brought to a minimum number only if the dietetic rules are followed as far as practicable, and yoga asanas are practised regularly with patience. Idleness is known to be one of the greatest hindrances of yoga. Everybody should practise yoga keeping an eye to his health. Diet is again, more important than practice of Yoga especially when the object is to uproot a particular disease.

Fast food which is catching up fast with the young generation is also the cause of many diseases. God knows better, how such misguiding ideas crop up in a human mind. The rule of cooking food is that food should be prepared slowly and not fast. It should be cooked on a low temperature. The fire too should be wooden and not gas, electric or kerosene oil which is injurious to health. If a research is done on the nutritive value of both the kinds of food – fast food and the food cooked with wooden fuel, it is sure the former would be proved to be of less nutritive value.

Ignorant people are carried away by advertisements and by repeatedly treading on the wrong path, the wrong path itself is mistaken for the right one. This is Kali Yuga; except love and life, everything seems to be possible by way of money. The wrong paths of human life are looked upon as fashion or an inescapable way of life in some cases. A vast majority of human beings have lost their common sense to look into the affairs of the world in its proper perspective. The reason is non-practice of Yoga and spirituality and, therefore, unveiling of spiritual acumen. Habitual use of heavily artificial or poisonous foods could be another formidable reason for such wrong notions. Despite all these misconceptions, may God bless them. Wrong food is the root biological cause for all the nefarious activities we come across through the mishaps taking place all over the world.

Swarga Ashram, **Swami Durganand Saraswati**
Rishikesh, Uttrakhand   durgamom2000@yahoo.co.in

1. History of Yogasanas

Asanas were derived from the 'Directions of the Unmanifest', the 'origin of all becomings.' When the Sages underwent severest variety of austerities in and around the caves of the Himalayas – a place where the Aryan Sages had settled down (from a central part of Asia) they faced many unbearable physical complaints, because the caves were bereft of any sunshine, full of humidity or unhygienic elements of Nature. The Sages pondered or in other words, prayed silently to the Almighty who directed the processes, names, rules and regulations through divine oracles – the facts in which some wise lucky yoga-doers have an intuitive experience. Thus, Yoga descended upon the earth from heaven for the good of one and all alike. Any human being who can think, can meditate and perform yoga unless he is absolutely bedridden or handicapped. Caste, creed, colour, religion, sex, nationality or dogmas are meaningless and lame excuses.

Practical Process

During the run of asanas, the anus, mouth and the eyes should be kept closed as per directions of the *Srimad Bhagwad Gita*. The holy scripture directs: "*Sarva Dwaranee Sangyamya....*" which means 'by restraining (the activities of) all the pores of the senses." The same scripture advises, *Nawa Dwar – a - Pur – a – Dehi* (a human body has nine pores of senses; but the supra sensory perception lies (unattached) within and without the nine doors (pores) of senses...)

Experience reveals the fact that the said process of restraining the senses works better for concentration which has a direct link with the hygiene of the meditators' economy too. The student or the reader should bear this in mind.

Definition of Asanas

According to Sri Sri Patanjali Maharishi, asanas may be defined as a physiological prayer that continues for quite a satisfactory amount of time and gives "comfort and stability. Thus, movement while performing a posture is not allowed except for preparatory stages only. In the actual state of a posture or an asana, stability or stillness of body is most desired on the ground that physiological reactions of a posture takes place inside the body only when breathing is withheld. To clarify, only the stabilised state of a pose can hold the air in check, and the effect of asanas starts working internally. Therefore, to give an example, if the Lotus Pose is done only for a few minutes, it is almost of no use at all to affect the body. According to ancient scriptures, one can claim a good command over a pose if one sticks to it for a time which should be about "three hours and forty eight minutes." It may sound almost impossible to some, but the sages used to maintain this time and even more than this.

Definition of a Mudra

Some mudras have been brought to the list of postures by the sages on the ground that the mudras function like asanas.

Different mudras affect different parts of the human body in a special way. To cite an example, Khechari Mudra has its powerful effect on mind. It teaches that there is nothing in this world except the sap of nothingness. Physiologically speaking, the mudra helps the tongue to extract the nectar to be oozed from the palate. Even as a bird flies in the air which is full of vacuity, so the mind when it is bereft of any thought, on matter or senses, enjoys the freedom, emancipation, liberation or riddance as a bird enjoys. This is the idea of the Khechari Mudra. The word mudra is a metaphor of the word ' coin'.

History of Yogasanas

Various Kinds of Asanas

There are some asanas which strengthen both the external and the internal parts of the body – to cite an example, the sunsalutation pose (also called dog forward and backward) and sitting standing (also called squatting). The former has a lot of internal effects on the human body.

Some have a serious effect on the functioning of the brain; e.g. the headstand pose, head between the legs pose, yoga mudra, triangular closure pose or peacock pose, etc. Some asanas look easy but have a beautiful and an important effect on the body. There are some asanas which are super classic, and the effects are priceless, e.g. matsendrio pose, liberation pose, and, tarasan, etc.

Still there are some which are difficult to achieve, but its effect is not so internal but external only, e.g. lifted lotus pose.

Most of the asanas are not meant for meditation direct, but are only a preparation for meditation en route purification of naris – a fact which the sages have termed kaya shuddhi (body purification). The following are the poses for meditation, because these poses help the human physiology to get the vital forces run into the central passage of the backbone and are more effective than any other postures.

In order of preference:
1. Siddhasana (may be called success pose)
2. Half cow mouth pose
3. Goraksha pose
4. Expansion of legs (a wise austerity pose indeed)
5. Ordinary pose (also called Sukhasana). Choice of preference differs from one doer to another.

Variation Postures

Any student can make a variation pose by employing the common sense. Variations can be discovered only if a little intelligence is applied. The variation poses which, in most cases, do not hit

Speaking of Curing Diseases through Yoga

the aim of the poses have not been dealt with elaborately for the purpose of restraining the volume of this book.

It is better to try to avoid the variation poses and to follow the poses direct as much as possible on the ground that despite imperfection in the beginning days only, the imperfect postures too would be of much help to solve the concerned problems. The imperfect postures themselves could be termed as variation postures. For instance, even if the peacock pose could not be done in the beginning days perfectly, the pressure which would be created in the belly can claim a beneficial return. It is, therefore, instructed not to follow various kinds of variation postures and to kill the precious time. The number of postures described in the book, if done regularly are guaranteed remedies against fighting any ailments both physiological and psychological.

However, the guidance of a demonstrator teacher is a wisest way to avoid probable adverse results arising out of doing a wrong yoga asana.

Lethargy, in the first instance, despair, nervousness, irregularity, etc. are hurdles of asanas which become nicer or perfect only after a period of time. To improve the effect of yoga, living on liquid foods especially at night is the best way. Fasting, however, is another.

Beginners should stop practising yoga (of asanas) after performing regularly for a number of days, if they feel pain in different parts of the body. After a gap of a few days, they should start again and increase slowly.

A homoeopathic remedy against pain in any part of the body – ARNICA-200 (made in Germany or U.S.A.) is of a great help to avert the problem of pain (two or three drops maximum on an empty stomach in 48 hours). The remedy could even be used twice a week for some weeks to mitigate the body pain. Instead of the morning dose, it could also be taken before bed time, the result is the same. Empty stomach is a better way.

History of Yogasanas

Food stands in the way of proper development. The aspirant or the patient should not be avaricious. To cite a scriptural maxim, the Mother in the form of a violent Administrator beats the tongue of a demon. The fact, however, teaches that greed for food or slip of tongue that could be a cause for a great violence should be restrained.

Restraining of lower senses, tongue, etc. has therefore, been adjudged by the sages as the first step towards practising or starting Yoga. No one can expect a desired results while violating these rules.

Total Number of Asanas

Some scriptures claim that the total number of asanas is eighty four hundred thousand. As per Yogai theory of evolution, human species came into being after evolving through the said member. Each species has therefore been looked upon as having a form from unicellular, e.g. amoeba, hydra, etc. to multi-cellular creatures. The form of each creature is looked upon as a pose and, hence, the said number of asanas. But the theory of evolution is, however, now a controversial issue.

However the scripture jumps from the said number to about one hundred or so. The said number, therefore, is a metaphor expression. By cutting down the number by and by, there are about one hundred postures that can cover all kinds of diseases. While trimming the number by and by, only a few postures are treated as meditation poses – success pose, goraksha pose, lotus pose and half cow mouth pose and ordinary pose. All these postures are connected with the rise of the Kundalini mainly. These poses are both spiritual and hygienic but this book deals with various kinds of physical complaints especially.

That the number of Asanas has been cut short to a few has a theological ground: gross Karma (work) of senses being finer and finer, the movements of the body are not needed so much when the Kundalini is awakened in the human body. Deep meditators can feel it intuitively. One should continue asanas till the rise of Kundalini.

The more the Kundalini rises, the more the meditator penetrates into the inner worlds where gross senses – hands, feet, eyes, nose, ears etc. do not function, but the mind is absorbed in the Absorption of the Absolute in proportion to the stages(chakras) the lucky has reached. The depths vary from one meditator to another in proportion to his good Karma- the best way to understand esoteric Dharma.

The greatest boon of Yoga is that it kills (reaches) two birds with one stone – both the birds – the Being and the becoming – seem to be equally strong – unlike other systems of ontology, namely, Bhakti (devotion), Gyan (discrimination), Karma (Selfless services), etc. Under the Sun, no system of religion is so hygienic, therapeutic and healthful as the Yoga system of the Aryan Sages. In many Western countries thousands of dollars have to be spent to maintain Health Insurance Scheme. Sincere yoga practitioners can easily avert a huge cost of health automatically.

In this book only those asanas that have a special relationship with physical complaints have been dealt with utmost honesty, sincerity and carefulness so that both the patients and the aspirants can extract the beneficial results of holy Yoga.

As for food, neither tea nor egg is an item of a yogic diet. Egg has no carbohydrate value. Only few naturopaths advocate this food. The ancient Yogis have not recommended it. Tea or coffee, in fact, are corrosive for liver. They kill the appetite and should not be taken on an empty stomach. Two or three glasses of water can be taken before having coffee or tea. Tea, however, should neither be hot nor cold – both the kinds are injurious to the teeth. These are some rules which should be followed by those who cannot go without tea or coffee.

It is imperative to follow the path of Yoga by giving up the bad habits of alcohol, tobacco, eating meat, smoking, etc. gradually Alcohol and meat-eating should be kicked out from life as soon as possible. Smoking a few times, however, is allowable in the

History of Yogasanas

beginning days of practice, but narcotics, *hashish* and the likes are highly injurious to the functioning of brain and lungs.

My attempt is trash, but I would, however, remain grateful to the practitioners if they are benefited by following the most practical systems laid down in the book.

May this book serve as a printed Guru!

Long Live Yoga!

Om! Peace, Peace, Peace

2. Asanas Helpful in Digestion

Vajra, a Sanskrit word stands for firmness. 'Asana' is derived from the word 'Aseen' which means to be, or to become or maintain. According to the **Bhagwad Gita** asana means – to be indifferent.

Vajrasana

Vajrasana

Procedure

1. Kneel down.
2. Now sit down on your heels maintaining a little gap. But the knees should be adjacent to each other.
3. Now, put both your hands on the knees by straightening your palms and fingers.
4. Breathe normally, inhaling and exhaling continuously.
5. Keep your eyes closed. This pose is performed by the yogis immediately after a heavy meal.

Other techniques being the same, this asana can also be done by maintaining a little distance between the heels. It is only a matter of variation but the result is the same. Some variations are necessary to break the monotony.

Asanas Helpful in Digestion

If this posture is maintained by bending the neck a little towards the front side, it may make a tribundh ('Tri' – three and 'bundh' – closure). Thus, tribundh is a closure of three parts of the body - first, moolbundh (closure of anus), second uddiyan (navel part) and the third is the den lying at the centre of the throat (throat den). The heat generated by this bundh is helpful for the body.

Curative Values

1. This asana is helpful in digestion if done after having food.

2. This asana helps create heat required by the pancreas to digest food.

3. Certain reports reveal the fact that it is a guard against sleep. Students requiring sleeplessness for a period of hours, unless the body is heavily weary, may try this pose and remain awake for some hours at least. Standing position of the body is also a guard against sleepiness.

4. People suffering from knee problems or those unable to sit in the lotus pose for a desired period of time would definitely be benefited by this pose.

5. This pose tries to compensate for the deformities of the body structure – a balanced proportion of sizes of the different parts of the body – shoulder, chest, waist, posterior and leg muscles.

6. If this pose is performed regularly (by keeping the feet a little apart), it will serve as a guard against excitement of lower nature (sex) immediately and the doer would be saved from arthritic (knee-joint) and sciatic diseases too.

The best way of maintaining this pose, say, for half an hour, is to keep one's mind engaged in reading a book while sitting in this pose so that time passes out unmindfully. This rule has been proved efficacious for many postures. In order to avoid sleep, one should maintain abstemiousness (avoiding things which give pleasure especially food), avoid starch food - rice, lentils, etc. and

Speaking of Curing Diseases through Yoga

too much of menial work. So far as knowledge goes, Muslims have adopted this pose for praying to Allah.

Lastly, as for digestion, there are other poses, which will be discussed in detail later in the book.

Care and Caution

- Keep the back erect perfectly.
- Keep your eyes always closed.
- Maintain closure of the anus (for the purpose of acquiring introversion slowly).
- The head should be slightly bent forward (to make the tribundh a success).

Temporary Protective Remedies

- Mince ginger and add some lemon juice and a pinch of rock salt (not common salt). Have this an hour before a meal every day.
- Ordinary stomach disorders can be corrected by eating a pinch (3 gms) of black pepper mixed with a pinch of rock salt before going to bed.
- According to an ancient scripture *Shivaswarodaya*, in case of a headache, the elbows should be tied with a piece of cloth or a rope. When the headache subsides untie the knot. The same process is applicable to sunshine headache, which continues till the sun shines. However, if it recurs, then close one nostril with your index finger and keep inhaling from the other nostril till the headache subsides.
- Having ginger before a meal is useful in digestion.

3. Leg Troubles

Two words, namely *Soo* and *Asti* make one word *Swasti* or *Swastik*. *'Soo'* means good, and *Asti*, to live, therefore, Swastik means to live well. Swastik is an auspicious symbol of the Vedas, although the symbol is misunderstood by some Westerners on the ground of historical facts. The pose when done, looks like Swastik.

Swastikasana

Procedure
1. Sit in Sukhasana (ordinary pose).
2. Put the right foot on the left thigh in such a way so that the heel of the left foot touches the genitals.

Swastikasana

Benefits
- This asana is helpful in overcoming the fidgets.
- Problem of sweaty palms and feet could be rectified through this pose.

Home Remedies
- Three glasses of hot water mixed with two or three lemons should be used for fomenting the legs and the rest of the mixture should be used to wash the soles of the feet.

- Only lemon juice also helps to remedy sweaty palms and feet.

Other Remedies

- Dog forward and sunsalutation, shoulder stand (sarvangasana) for a number of times is helpful.
- Massaging by striking all the parts of the leg gently and not with too much force can mitigate the pain to a great extent.
- Trifala, an Ayurvedic remedy, accompanied with a homoeopathic medicine should serve the purpose.
- Sitting standing as well as cycling will help.
- Diet should not be starchy, especially at night. It is mentionable that an average student of Yoga practising regularly will hardly face this situation permanently. Having excess of salt and sugar is not healthy. Rock salt is better than the common salt.

Care and Caution

- Chest should be expanded.
- Keep your eyes closed.
- Head should be bent slightly. The hands could be kept either on the knees or on the lap according to one's convenience.

4. Lack of Confidence

Confidence is badly required to face an examination, interview, undertaking any exploration, or a business project, etc. Yogasanas and pranayamas boost up one's morale day-by-day. There is a no exaggeration in it.

Singhasana (Lion Pose)

This pose resembles a lion (perhaps). There is a part of the body which is fleshy and paddy but a little hardy inside – situated one inch above the front side of the anus. Scriptures name it Dehamadhya or perineum. The hard part inside this paddy flesh is called *sibni nari* through which semen flows.

Procedure

1. Squat on the toes in such a way so that the heels press the sibni nari.
2. Keep the knees at a distance of about one foot from each other.
3. Try to look in between your eyebrows. You can also gaze at the tip of the tongue. The result has been reported to be same.
4. Take out (exhibit) your tongue fully.
5. Maintain this posture for some time.

Singhasana (Lion Pose)

Physiotherapeutic Benefits

- As the name lion suggests, the Yogi acquires abundant mental stamina, patience, tolerance and, above everything else, fearlessness. This asana uproots fear, psychosis nervousness, unrighteousness, timidity and narrow mindedness. This pose looks funny but has no doubt a tremendous psychic value.
- Physiologically, this asana is helpful in maintaining a good dental health. Regular practice of this asana with moolbundh will automatically ensure tribundh.
- This asana also increases physical strength to a great extent. The sages have deciphered and designed the Yoga postures in such a way that they bring forth both chivalry and introversion at one and the same time.

Care and Caution

Your heels may skid from the sibni nari – the central subject of the pose. Therefore do the posture carefully.

5. Loss of Spirit

Veerasana

Veer denotes indomitability, courage and invincibility, etc. Like the singhasana just described in the previous chapter, the regular practice of veerasana enables the practitioner to fight unrighteousness or negativities with an absolute spirit of candidness, neutrality and tolerance. This pose is, however, not so important for meditation.

Procedure

1. Kneel down.
2. Step forward your left leg while the other should be stretched out behind.
3. Left arm should be straightened with the hand closed, while the other hand should be kept folded and kept behind the back.
4. Stare any object or the blue sky with eyes wide open.
5. Maintain the pose for some time.
6. Repeat the pose with the other leg also.

Veerasana

Benefits

Remedy against nervousness

- Only people with a weak, unhealthy heart are victims of mental weakness. As for the aspirants of Nothingness (Non-duality), in order to improve the possibility, one should chalk out one's own defects and repeat these words to yourself again and again. "I will make it a success, come what may". This mantra should be repeated at least 10,000 times while doing the asana. There is one more posture at least by which one could be highly benefitted, i.e the Kalbhairavi posture. This posture is almost equally powerful or more than veerasana.

- Regular practice of this asana accompanied with a strict diet and the advice from an Ayurvedic teacher will serve the purpose. Idleness and oversleeping, etc. will be removed. The doer should be very careful to see if he is constipated.

True Yoga spirit is connected with the Satvik. Yoga practitioners purge out the impurities of their minds and attain the 'Spirit' at the end of all Yoga actions – Asana, Pranayamas etc. The readers especially the Yoga practitioners are advised not to mistake 'spirit' for the strength of self-conceit or muscle power. One should possess muscle power through Yoga of Sun-salutations, etc. but it should be utilised for self-defence, if need be and for the upliftment of one's own little self-suffering from nescience.

In fact, with the gradual rise of the Power Dormant which has been described by poets as the Kundalini Mother, the doer feels a buoyant spirit even when he walks along the road. Unluckily, a group of misguided Western yoga practitioners misuse this 'buoyant spirit' in enjoying sensual pleasures recklessly by mistake and, thus, lose, the real fruit of Yoga.

6. Night Pollution

Guptasana

Procedure
1. Sit on the ground.
2. Fold your left leg to the extent that the heel touches the anus.
3. Now put the right leg on the left thigh.
4. The situation would be such that the *sibni nari* of the *dehamadhya* (one inch above the anus front side) is rigidly pressed by the heel which has been placed close to the anus.

Guptasana

(Intelligent readers must have marked that the asanas-especially the important ones have a connection with the base of the spinal cord.)

Benefits

When the dehamadhya is pressed, a kind of heat is created. The heat enables the wind or the air of the body to rise up. This in fact lifts up the wind (or mind) of the doer to go up and not think about the lower senses.

Speaking of Curing Diseases through Yoga

- Maintenance of celibacy is a possibility by this pose.
- Seminal defects are thus removed.
- Night pollution as well as urinary diseases, etc. are checked if this pose is practised regularly.

Remedies

- Either meditate on God, do japa or close your eyes and maintain silence just before lying down on the bed. The period depends on your own capacity and the amount of time in hand. Have one more glass of cold water before going to bed.
- Don't pamper your senses.
- Keep your stomach unconstipated, free from any complaints.
- Avoid food that creates heat in the stomach.
- Avoid eating at late hours in the night.
- Use Triphala (an Ayurvedic medicine).
- Homoeopathic remedies can also be taken.
- Don't allow anyone to sleep with you.
- Practice of Moolbundh helps a lot.
- Meat, egg, alcoholic beverages welcome this complaint. So avoid having them.
- Padangusthasana is also helpful.
- Spinach cools down the stomach and is helpful to fight this problem. However, it should not be consumed during rainy season or at night.
- One or half a teaspoon of liquorice powder mixed with a teaspoon of honey helps to combat this disease.
- Before going to bed legs and groin should be washed with cold water.

Night Pollution

Strict celibacy calls for taking bath twice or even thrice a day. If night pollution takes place once or twice a month between the age group of 25 and 45, it is not very harmful.

Powdered basil seeds (5gms) mixed with cold water or coconut oil makes another remedy. The mixture should be taken before going to bed for some days.

It should be remembered that all the yoga postures in which the backbone stands erect can help create Tribundh (closure of anus, naval part of the belly and the den of the throat called kanthakoop in Sanskrit) only after some days of regular practice.

Padangusthasana

Pad means leg and *Angushta*, fingers or toes. Hence the name padangusthasana as the entire body stays on the toes.

Procedure

- Sit on the toes.
- The heel must press the Dehamadhya.
- Fold the right leg and keep it on the left thigh.
- Keep the back straight.
- Look forward but (with eyes closed) pay attention to the Dehamadhya.
- Set the hands to the sides of your waist.
- Maintain balance.

Padangusthasana

Angustha Nasasparshasana

This posture is highly useful for night pollution. Moreover, the pose helps to maintain good health of the eyes and anus-related complaints. You may call it the toe kissing pose also.

Angustha Nasasparshasana

Procedure

- Lie down on the ground.
- Take the left foot up towards the chin holding it with both the hands.
- Try to stay in this position for sometime. Then relax and repeat the same process with the other leg also.

7. Fearfulness

Kal Bhairav, as mentioned earlier is a demonic manifestation of the Almighty, symbolising a bold attitude of the image of a God named 'Bhairav' whose complexion is as black as coal, and whose main nature is to destroy and annihilate everything. He has a fearless attitude towards anything and everything. It should be borne in mind that fear is also a kind of hindrance to Yoga. Timid people consume a lesser amount of oxygen than the fearless ones whose heart functions much better than those who fear. *Kal* is an indication of time or death in Sanskrit.

Kal Bhairav

Procedure

- Stand on the ground. Put one leg forward about one and a half feet in front. The other leg should remain at the same place.
- Extend one hand forward and one towards the back.
- Open your mouth and take your tongue out fully.
- Try to look in between the eyebrows.
- Maintain this posture with an emotion awaiting the devastating power (devastation of falsehood, unrighteousness or negativities).

- Do it again and again by changing the legs.

Sitting standing too should be done double the dog forward or backward. Generally between 25 and 50 one should perform minimum 50 dog forwards and also sitting standing accordingly (about 100).

Benefits

- This pose works as a guard against torpidity or lethargy.
- Regular practice of this asana with an observance of strict diet will guarantee fearlessness. The conclusion is open to experimental verification. The time required varies from one practitioner to another because everybody's state is not as same as another.
- This asana has a prophylactic aspect too. It is helpful in maintaining good dental health. It is helpful in improving the eyesight. The pose should be done by changing the legs.

Remedies

- Take Triphala twice a day after dinner.
- Abstain from sexual activities.
- Knee stand pose and nervous pose are also highly useful.
- "I am not afraid of anyone or anything, come what may" – should be uttered for about an hour at a stretch especially before going to bed.

Diet

- Gourd, mint, raisins and grapes should be consumed. Gourd jukinee is said to be highly effective for bringing forth courage and mental strength.
- Garlic juice, ginger juice, sugar candy or honey – all these have to be mixed and should be taken (two spoonfuls) twice a day.

Fearfulness

- Half cow mouth pose is another great helpful physiological remedy.
- In most of the cases when someone is afraid of seeing something – three cups of plain water mixed with salt (common salt or rock salt) works very well.

8. Headache and Related Problems

Headache, migraine and dizziness – are all caused by disorderly functioning of the brain. As for psychological factors, unwise thinking, unreasonableness, improvident insight, attachment to excessive mundane thoughts are the main cause of this complaint for which patients spend a lot of money on allopathic remedies which only suppress the complaint for sometime but do not cure the problem permanently.

Head Between Legs Pose

Procedure

- Stand astride with both the legs about two and a half feet apart from each other.
- Bend forward slowly trying to hold the legs with your hands.
- Now bend more taking your shoulders and head behind your legs.
- Try to reach up as far as you can holding your legs looking up towards the sky so that your navel could be sighted by a bystander.

Head Between Legs Pose

- Stay in this pose till you feel pain in the backbone.
- Repeat this.
- Practise this pose regularly, gradually increasing its duration.

Remedies

- Have Triphala, Goolkand Safi or Isabgol to keep your stomach cleaned.
- Dog forward and sun salutations should be done once or twice a day.
- Other helpful asanas are-head stand pose, peacock pose, Full Matsyendrasana or half Koormasana (tortoise pose) are also helpful.
- Toning and massaging of body especially the head is also helpful.

Do's & Don'ts

- Relax yourself mentally.
- Don't indulge in sexual activities excessively.
- Drink a lot of water.
- The patient should not be constipated at all.
- Pungent spices especially dry red chilly should be avoided.
- Non-vegetarian food – meat, alcoholic beverages should not be taken.

Home Remedies

- Take the juice of the leaves of carrot which is cooked in moderate fire and drop it in the ear and nose.
- Putting a few drops of the juice of the leaves of lemon into the nostrils is helpful to relieve headache and migraine.

- About 15 leaves of basil mixed with around 10 grains of black pepper, if drunk during the running condition, helps to subside the pain to a great extent.
- Jamun (an Indian fruit) or berry should be eaten in the morning as a curative remedy against headache which occurs only in the day time.

Obesity

Lack of physical work and excessive amount of food especially the stuff that creates fat in the body are the two main causes of obesity.

Remedies

- The first remedy is to stop eating solid foods and live mostly on liquid foods excluding milk and milk products. Have mainly vegetable and fruit juices.
- Engage yourself in some physical activity like running, walking, jogging or dog forward and backward.
- Navel exercise (Nauli).
- Breathing exercises.
- Ayurvedic medicine combined with homoeopathic ones.
- Reduce the frequency of sexual activities.
- Regular practice of an intensive Yoga exercise is also a solution – three hours in the morning and two hours in the evening. There is no better natural way than this.
- Obesity is a word which is out of the dictionary of a sincere and regular Yoga practitioner. Sun salutation and squatting twice a day accompanied with dietetic rules, e.g. living mostly on liquid food especially vegetable juice, fruit juice, lemon juice, orange juice, etc. is also highly fruitful.
- Fasting with no water is injurious to health.

Headache and Related Problems

Sun Salutation

- Paschimottanasana, peacock pose, wheel pose, mahamudra, half and full koormasana (tortoise) pose, nauli, etc. are highly effective. However, a reasonable quantity of honey and lemon juice with hot water should be taken every day as it helps to cut down fat. The slimming process should not be fast but slow which is natural and not harmful to the body.

9. Hernia

Hernia is a medical condition in which an organ pushes through the muscle which surrounds it. Uneven distribution of wind or air in the economy is the root cause of hernia.

The patient should never be constipated. It is better to live on water or fruit juices only and nothing else during the acute state.

Homoeopathic and Ayurvedic medicines work a lot. The acute state can also be treated by the following posture.

Janushirsasana

Procedure

- Sit down on the floor stretching out the legs extending them forward.
- Now stretch both legs wide apart and fold one leg.
- Set the heel of the folded leg on the spot of the pain.
- Catch with both hands all the toes of the other leg.
- Make sure that enough pressure is exerted on the spot of the pain.
- Repeat the process with the other leg also.

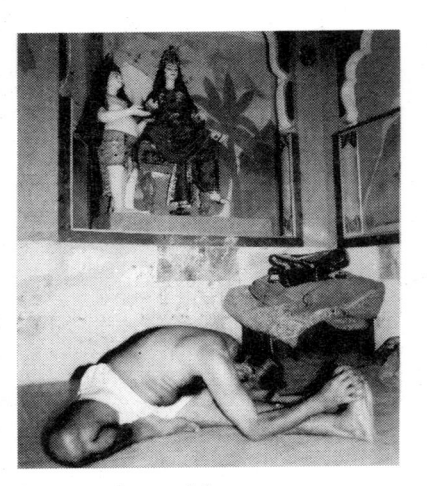

Janushirsasana

Hernia

Remedies

- To undergo a surgical operation is not unwise but if yoga is not done regularly with observance of dietetic rules, the complaints are sure to attack again.
- To guard against wind, use some ginger and black pepper in fruit juices. Triphala should be consumed thrice a day in an acute state. It should also be taken twice a day permanently for general health.
- Shirsasana (headstand) has a great effect. Pawanmuktasana is a special posture. Yoga mudra is equally important.
- Diet must not be wind-creating. Hot fomentation in an acute condition is effective. Hot rice poultice is highly beneficial.
- Intensive yoga exercises.
- Magnet therapy works especially in pain related complaints like this. Cow mouth pose, matsyendra pose and peacock pose are all useful postures.
- While doing the yogamudra in case of acute condition, the patient or doer should press the navel with his fist nicely bend down to touch the ground for a period of time. At other times try to catch the toes and make the backbone bent to the point of the ground. The stay should continue for about 15 minutes to derive the desired results. Janushirasana is almost the same as Mahamudra except that the heel in the Janushirasana should be placed on the spot of the pain and in the Mahamudra, the heels should be placed on the Dehamadhya – one inch above the anus (front side). The two poses almost look alike.

10. Wind in the Stomach (Tympanitis)

According to Ayurveda, an imbalance of any one of these – Kaph, Pitta and Vayu is the root cause of any disease. Breathing exercises done in a lotus pose or meditation in the success pose also works for this purpose.

Vayu or air is of two types. The first variety does not have an offensive smell and therefore, is not so bad for the time being, although regular formation of air encroaches the unwanted passages, arteries and veins of the human body and causes many diseases like arthritis, sciatica, knee joint diseases, etc. So, the formation of excessive wind should not be allowed to happen.

The second variety of wind smells odious as this is caused by indigestion of food. This wind is called gas. Sweating labour, vigorous yoga exercises, namely, dog forward and backward and sitting standing, peacock pose, matsyendra pose, headstand, scorpion or tree pose, success (siddha) pose, lotus pose and long time retentive breathing exercises are certainly curative. The Indian system of passing stool is highly hygienic, thanks to the guidelines of the ancient sages. The Indian system of toilet itself is actually pawanmuktasana.

Ardh Koomarasana (Half tortoise pose)

Procedure

- Kneel down.
- Interlock your fingers and bring them closer to your navel and press it.

Wind in the Stomach (Tympanitis)

- Lean forward slowly to the extent to which you are comfortable.
- Try to touch the ground with your nose.
- Maintain the stay as long as it is comfortable.
- Other helpful poses are dead pose, hand stand pose, peacock pose, tree pose and scorpion pose and mandukasana.

Ardh Koomarasana (Half tortoise pose)

Home Remedies

- Drink one glass of tepid water mixed with half a teaspoon of either black salt or a pinch of asafoetida on an empty stomach.
- A combination of ginger and garlic powder and rock salt mixed in a glass of tepid or hot water works very well.
- Observance of Yogic asanas or sitting-standing, i.e. squatting and standing for many times will also serve the purpose as it stabilises breathing and drives out the unhygienic wind of the stomach.
- Acidity, gastritis can be brought to a halt by having tepid water, raw coconut, dry coconut or moong dal. A variety of lentils of India or Asia if chewed and eaten with water can be really helpful to relieve tympanitis.
- Raw moong dal should be put in water for about 30 minutes and should be eaten by chewing it.

11. Navel Displacement

It may happen accidentally or due to a heavy intake of food. It is a disease in which navel is displaced from its proper place. Navel being the central part of the human body, has arteries and veins which spread all over the body for proper functioning.

The patient experiences the need for relieving himself quite frequently, suffers from indigestion, uneasiness in the stomach, retching, etc. In addition to Uttanpadasana, the following postures are also beneficial: shoulder stand, boat pose, locust pose, half tortoise pose, camel pose, shirsasana (headstand), wheel pose, bow pose.

Supta Vajrasana

Procedure

1. Lie down on your back.
2. Set the back of your cranium on the ground and keep your legs folded as shown in the picture.

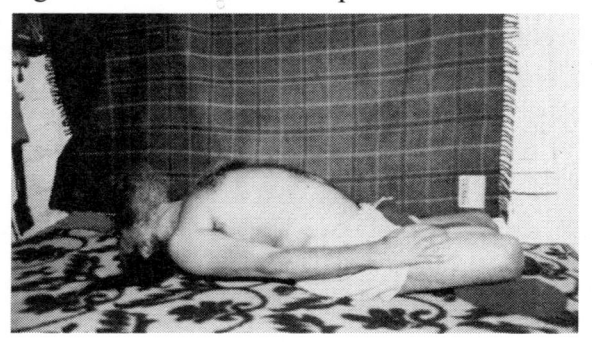

Supta Vajrasana

Navel Displacement

3. Try to lift your chest as high as you can.
4. Keep your hands at the thighs or a little under the thighs.
5. Maintain the stay for as long as you can comfortably.
6. Keep breathing normally all through the asana.

Note: Do it again and again until tired. Maintain the anal closure.

Supta vajrasana and naukasana (boat pose) are almost same, especially in regard to the effect of these poses on the navel part of the human constitution.

Benefits

- In addition to its effect on the navel, it has a good effect on the rise of the Kundalini and on the loss of appetite also. Spinal cord also becomes flexible.
- This pose has a great capacity to invigorate the fallen energy. It beats down inertness also.
- Uttanmandukasana is also a helpful pose for navel displacement.
- Boat pose is also called Purvoottanasana by some sages. If the boat pose is done in a reverse way or, in other words, by lying down on the navel and straightening the hands, then this helps cut down fats in the body.
- Kandapeerasana or liberation pose has recently been reported to be highly useful for this problem.
- Preparatory shoulder stand is another beautiful pose to fight the same complaint. Preparatory shoulder stand is also called veepareet karani mudra.

Some Ayurvedic doctors are of the opinion that if the distance from the navel to the nipples of the breasts is not equal in case of male patients, then the person suffers from this problem and in case of females the same distances should be measured from the navel to the big toes of the legs. But this finding has not

Speaking of Curing Diseases through Yoga

been proved in all the cases. There may be some more factors to diagnose the complaint. But loose motions, retching, indigestion, pain or uneasiness, etc. are generally the common symptoms.

Finger Strengthening Pose

There are people whose fingers and legs move fast and tremble on account of weakness (of heart or of the entire economy). To overcome this problem it is wise to do a lot of Yoga postures including sweating labour or dog forward, etc. and at the same time take ayurvedic and/or Homoeopathic medicines. The patient is also advised not to indulge in sexual activities for some time. Fresh sea fish and river fish, etc. are highly strengthening as well as curative as fish contains iodine which is important for good health. In addition to the Tolangulasana, the remedy under discussion, the patient should use Triphala thrice a day. Consume milk, dried fruits, especially cashew nuts and follow the following postures especially:

Tolangulasana Pose (Finger Strengthening Pose)

Navel Displacement

- Dog forward and backward (Sun Salutation)
- Sitting standing (Squatting)
- Peacock pose
- Wheel pose
- Matsyendra pose
- Tree pose
- Scorpion pose
- Head stand
- Navel exercise

As for fruits, grapes, papaya, radish, red beat, etc. are good. Breathing exercises, especially retentive breathing, is very much useful.

In the old books this pose has been given in a different way. Sit in lotus pose and put your hands in between the thighs. Now try to lift your body with the help of your hands. This can be done only when the hands are strong.

12. Sensual Thoughts

The word Brahmacharya is constituted by two words 'brahm' and 'acharya'. Brahma means 'the Almighty Omnipotent' and Acharya means 'who behaves in that manner'. Thus, Brahmacharya means an aspirant who behaves for the purpose of attainment of the Brahma (Self, Almighty, Supreme Being…). The action of the aspirant is what is called Brahmacharya.

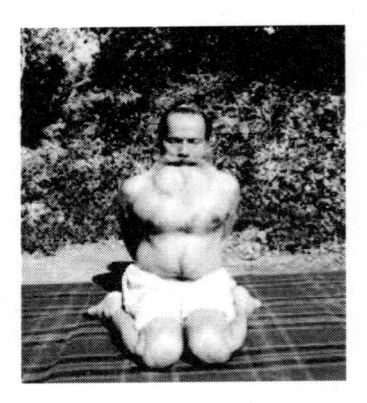

Brahmacharyasana

Brahmacharyasana

Let us break the monotony of harping the words 'diseases' and listen to a historical story of India.

Once upon a time a king asked one of his courtiers Gopal Bhar whose duty it was to amuse the king and his fellows with jokes, humours, etc., "Well! Gopal Bhar', reply to my question within two days and if you fail to satisfy me with your answer, not only your services will be dispensed with, but also you will be beheaded. The question was – till what age this dormant desire after lower senses continue in the human body? At which age does it stop?"

The word "Bhar" means buffoon. Gopal Bhar came back to his house. He forgot his meal, fell into a pensive mood, turned pale and passed the night absolutely without sleep. Early in the morning his daughter, a lady of wisdom, came to serve tea and was astonished to see his plight.

Sensual Thoughts

The daughter assured him of a satisfactory reply without fail. Gopal took the meal with a spirit half-broken. Next day, his daughter presented him a bowl of soil and taught her father that the bowl full of soil was the answer to the king's question. She also explained it to her father in brief.

Next day Gopal went to the king and told him that as long as palpitation of heart continues, sensual inclination will be there. It is only when we die, when we are transformed into soil that our sensual feelings also die. This bowl full of soil is an indication of this harsh reality. It is samadhi only that can help a man to overcome the feelings of sensuality. Gopal told the king that his daughter explained this to him. The king was very impressed. He summoned his daughter, patted her back and rewarded her.

The western devotees who are sincerely willing to maintain celibacy should practise following methods:

- Try to avoid sensual environment.
- Have a glass of cold water when attacked by a sensual excitement.
- Avoid overeating and consuming alcohol. Drink plenty of cold water and eat in moderation.
- Eat only vegetarian food.

This pose is almost like vajrasana. The only difference is that the feet should be kept at a distance of about one foot from the buttock while the hands should be taken at the back and fingers are interlocked. This pose like Vajrasana could be done after having meals too. The best way to continue or maintain this stay in this pose is to read books while doing it so that time passes out a little easily. Thus the time of staying would increase slowly.

Other Helpful Poses

- Expansion of legs (Dwipada vistrita asana)
- Success pose (Siddhasana)
- Half cow mouth pose

Speaking of Curing Diseases through Yoga

All these postures guarantee beating down sensuality at least for a period of time. The best way is to meditate or do Japa for about half an hour before going to bed. It can also be done while sitting on the bed.

A good degree of celibacy is maintained only by full-fledged sincere aspirants, and not by the half-hearted souls.

13. Improvement of IQ

Matsyendrasana

Procedure
- Sit down on the floor and fold your right leg in such a way that the heel touches the groin.
- Lift the left leg and place it across the right leg.
- Take your right hand from outside the left leg and try to hold the right feet. The left hand should be placed at the back by folding it.
- Turn your back and head towards the left as far as possible.
- Do the same process on the other side as well.

Matsyendrasana

Other Helpful Poses Connected with I.Q.
- Meditate in dwipada vistritasana at least two or three times a day.

Speaking of Curing Diseases through Yoga

- Head stand pose (the time of staying should be increased while restraining from sex or at least doing it in moderation).
- Matsyendrasana
- Karnapeerasana
- Maintenance of silence each day or on a particular day for some time (This is very important).
- Cut down social relationships as much as possible.

Diet

The diet should not cause any complaint in the body. The diet should be yogic as much as possible. Egg, meat, tobacco and alcoholic items are not congenial and are injurious to the normal functioning of the brain. Drinking large quantities of vegetable juices is also beneficial.

Other Helpful Measures

- The aspirant should play chess or try to work out mathematical problems every day. This has been experimentally verified.
- Clarified butter made from pure cow's milk is helpful in improving I.Q. Eating fish is also good for the brain. The fish products should be fresh.
- One should indulge in various sports activities like volley ball, cricket, football, etc.
- Stomach should be kept neat and clean and, therefore, Triphala should be consumed twice a day.
- Padangustha pose is highly useful for everyone as it protects and conserves the vital fluid of the human body.
- Carrot is also said to be very much useful in this complaint.

14. Improving Concentration

Poets have described the human mind in so many ways. Some say it is a fish out of water, others have compared it to the restlessness of a dozen monkeys tempted by two bananas, if the bananas are not given to them but are used for tantalisation. Theologists call it the first Spandan Atmika Maya - the Supreme Being is absolutely still and the mind is the first vibration generated by the Almighty's power of illusion - non-existent existence of this scenic world. All sensorial objects, however, belong to Maya.

The following postures and methods have been found to be very efficacious:

Siddhasana (Success Pose)

Procedure

- Sit erect.
- Set the back side of the heel of the left leg to the spot lying only one inch above the anus, i.e. dehamadhya.
- See to it that the dehamadhya is nicely pressed while the hands could be kept on the lap or on the knees.

Siddhasana (Success Pose)

- Bend slightly towards the front side with eyes closed and most important with anus closed for as much time as you can and then release the anus. Take rest and do it again.
- Moolbandh (i.e, closure of the anus) should be maintained.

Speaking of Curing Diseases through Yoga

- The aspirant should now meditate on god, nature, or anything. You may chant hymns. You may also use the mantra given by your teacher. Repeated practices with successes and failures will gradually make you ingenious.

Now focus your attention on the following parts of the body:

- Toes
- Heels
- Legs
- Navel
- Central part of the chest (If you are an atheist, concentrate on your own image, if not, do it on the feet of your Deity and, if you are a non-dualist concentrate on the Supreme Unmanifest formless being).
- Throat-concentration to the central part of your throat Kanthakoop (in Sanskrit), or, throat den and then,
- Mouth
- Tongue
- Palate
- Centre part of the brows
- Crown of the head

A believer of God should concentrate much more on the central part of the chest than any other part of the body. Concentration on God could be substituted by one's material desires. Instead of crown, one may focus on the central part of one's eyebrows too. The ultimate result is the same.

Benefits

- Siddhasana is also a useful pose for the remission of ordinary fevers but the patient should sit in this pose for about an hour at least.
- Regular practice of this pose would ensure concentration of mind. This pose is meant especially for the development of mind.

Siddhasana or Success Pose

Diet

- Diet for meditation in any pose should be simple. As for quantity eat only half the stomach. The aspirant should follow the yogi dietetic rules as far as practicable.

The aspirant may also count the beads of a rosary, or in other words do japa in the pose. Siddhasana should be done after performing pranayama.

Expansion of Legs

This pose can be aptly called leg pain devastating pose. In old age people have problem moving around due to pain in their joints and legs but the yogis do not have any such problem. This pose is highly beneficial in relieving pain in legs.

Procedure

- Sit erect.
- Expand your legs on both sides.
- Put your hands on both the knees and try to move forward but be sure that the heels should not move even slightly.
- Day by day, your backbone will be set just parallel to the heels.

Expansion of Legs

- This is a bit difficult pose in the beginning but very comfortable, enjoyable and concentrating in the long run.
- In the beginning you can take the help of a wall by keeping your back against it and then extend your legs in the opposite direction.
- If for some practitioners this is absolutely impossible, they may take to Sukhasana (ordinary pose of sitting with the backbone erect and the anus closed) and concentrate on the body parts mentioned above. The result depends upon sincerity of the practitioner.

Other Remedies

- **Tratak:** Stare any object continuously as long as it is comfortable. This is a good exercise for the eyes. Tratak should be continued till water starts rolling down your eyes.
- Maintenance of silence is one effective way, while cutting down relationships with worldly affairs is another.
- Craving for sensual pleasures and attainment of realisation at one and the same time has never been advocated by any sage of the yore. No one can cross a river in two boats.
- Head stand, in addition to the said methods and daily yoga programmes can be recommended for better concentration.
- As for food, a heavy quantity of green vegetable juice (fenugreek, carrot, radish, spinach, red beat, etc.) is useful for improving concentration.
- The hair oil of the meditator should be Ayurvedic which has a cooling effect. Mahabringraj (Ayurvedic) oil is best for the meditator.
- The victim should be reserved and cut down sociability to the minimum.
- One should abstain from perpetrating negative activities.

15. Prophet Mohammad Yoga

Paschimottanasana

Allah knows it better why Prophet Mohammad did not explain the reason as to why Muslims take to the West for the purpose of performing their prayers which they call *namaz*. It may be that the time or the then social system was not congenial to explain the real fact of Yoga, which is a matter of internal physiology of man; but the prophet knew all about the Kundalini more or less.

Kundalini, a dormant serpent power, lies at the back of the spinal cord of human beings, means an unmicroscopic subtle power coiled around the main Nari or central invisible arterial passage. The mouth of the coil is at the west and not at the east. It has to be brought to the east by repeatedly doing this pose. The west (backside) if pressed, and irritated could turn right slowly and open up the mouth of the central passage connected with the Sushumna which has gone up towards the chest, head, etc. through the backbone. This is the reason why the Muslims perform namaz facing the West and not the East, so far as the knowledge goes. Yoga or Namaz has its prophylactic as well as healthful aspects, which are really astonishing. Has there been a religion, which is as good as hygienic or as scientific as Yoga? We should kiss the dust of the lotus feet of the seer sages of the yore countless times.

The reason as to why the Aryans, Hindus or Vedic aspirants face the East or the North is that the Sun, the supreme Authority of the Universe, whom the scientists term, 'the source of all energy' rises in the East. So the Aryans acquire the blessings (power) of the sun. As for the North, the reason is that the aspirant tries to annihilate the components of the material parts of his body (*Khiti*) and the 'Himalayas are the special manifestation of (*Vibhutis*) the Unmanifest (Srimad Bhagwad Gita). The aspirant starts with Khiti (the solid part of the economy), the other components of the human flesh and blood of any material being are *Apa* (water), *Teja* (fire), *Marut* (ether) and lastly, *Vayu* (air).

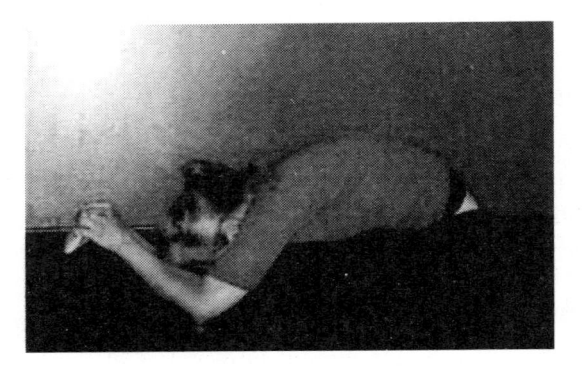

Paschimottanasana

Procedure

- Sit down on the floor.
- Extend your legs in front in a parallel position.
- Raise your hands up and now bend forward.
- Try to catch the toes of the feet.
- Don't try to strain yourself by reaching out for your toes if you are uncomfortable.

Benefits

- It makes the backbone supple.
- It strains the coil (as explained) so that the Kundalini Mother could be made active.
- This pose reduces obesity.
- It is a highly useful pose for making one introvert, if done for at least 15 minutes.

Prophet Mohammad Yoga

Finishing Paschimottanasana

- It removes depression and brings cheerfulness.
- This pose wards off complaints of the legs – pain, inflammation, arthritic problems, deformity of the legs, etc.
- The doer is saved from being attacked with skin diseases.
- Body odour as well halitosis can also be removed;

This pose needs to be done for a longer period of time – at least for half an hour without break. Paschimottanasana should be followed by a pose in which the back is bent backwards such as the wheel pose, snake or the bow pose.

It is absolutely unwise, hazardous or even dangerous to perpetrate any yoga pose without the guidance of a teacher. The teacher himself should be an ingenious demonstrator. Insanity, waywardness, loss of faith in Yoga – these are the outcome of violation of Yoga rules.

Care and Caution

- The hamstring or the tendons of the legs should be mercilessly strained.
- Catch all the fingers of the legs and not one or two.
- If it is difficult to catch the toes at the starting days, keep the legs straight and keep swinging forward and backward to make the performance a success.

The pose being done, the doer should finish the pose by being bending backwards with hands up and then following it with camel, snake, bow or wheel poses, etc. *Paschim* means west and *utthan* to lift up (strain) – hence the name is paschimottan pose.

Remedy: Study of scriptures is really helpful for attaining innerness. Cut down social relationships as much as possible.

16. Problem of Early Rising

Kookkootasana

Kookkoot means cock. As cock crows at dawn when the Yogis should get up from bed and start practising yoga, hence the name – Kookkootasana.

Procedure

- Sit in the lotus pose.
- Thrust your hands into the folded legs.
- The fingers of both the hands set to the ground should resemble the feet of a bird like duck, etc. There should be a gap between the fingers.

Kookkootasana

- Now, with all your strength lift up your body so much so that it goes above the elbows. This will happen gradually.
- Maintain the pose.

Benefits

- This pose in addition to the said benefits has a tremendous impact on the entire stomach, lungs, liver and heart and thereby works as an internal masseur.
- This pose helps to get up early in the morning.
- Strengthens the arms more and more. It is observed that females fail to lift up their bodies in the poses like dog

forward, etc. on account of their weak arms. Weakness of arms is caused by improper distribution of blood in different parts of the body or by a weak constitution.
- This pose is helpful in overcoming the fidgets.
- It makes a person more active and drives away lethargy.

Other Remedies
- Increase the intake of water. Avoid eating anything at night or have only liquid food.
- Meditate or perform Japa just before going to bed and continue doing it till you fall asleep (use an incense stick with a good fragrance).
- Sleep on your left hand side and not on the right as the alimentary canal lies on the left hand side only.
- Don't keep your hands on the chest while sleeping.
- Think something good, beautiful and enchanting before going to bed. Avoid taking negative thoughts to bed.
- Beware of constipation.

17. Deformities of Testicles or Related Problems

Men suffering from this complaint should give up on foods containing starch or which produce more water. They should fast on full moon, new moon and the eleventh day of both the new moon and the full moon. Either they should fast for 24 hours only on water or eat only once in the afternoon. Avoid eating anything at night. Milk or any other liquid or fruit juice can be consumed at night. Homoeopathic and Ayurvedic remedies work effectively.

Men suffering from this problem should indulge in certain physical activities or intensive Yoga practices. In addition to sankatasana, the following poses are recommended:

Gomukhasana (Cow Mouth Pose)

- Half cow mouth (It is similar to cow mouth pose or gomukhasana – except that the hands are set on the knee only). Make sure that the scrotum is nicely pressed. Stay in this pose for about half an hour each time. See to it that it works or not.
- Siddhasana or Success pose
- In an acute state brahmacharya pose could be beneficial.

Speaking of Curing Diseases through Yoga

- In an acute state, headstand also works although for sometime only.

Sankatasana

Procedure

- Stand erect.
- Lift one leg up and take it around the other leg, tactfully or ingeniously so that the testicle (which is deformed) is pressed heavily. The pressure should be increased steadily.
- Lift your arms up and take one hand behind the other and try to interlock the fingers.
- Repeat with the other leg too.

Garudasana (Garud is a kind of mythological bird) is also highly useful for diseases connected with testicles and/or scrotum.

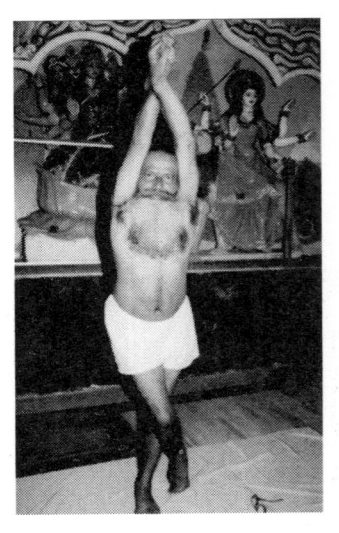

Sankatasana

Diet

Wind creating food and the food that cool down the stomach should be avoided. Dry fruits, honey, broken wheat, garlic (and not raw onion), etc. are congenial to remedy the complaint.

It is better to avoid food at night. Instead a little more quantity may be added to the usual daily diet in the afternoon. The complaint should not be allowed to reach an intractable state. Starch food, cabbage, cauliflower, radish, banana, orange, lemon, tomatoes, curd, etc. should be taken sparingly. Intake of garlic should be increased.

18. Senility

Senility is sure to attack the body gradually but if this pose is followed every day, senility can be beaten at least for about twenty years with the regular practice of chakra pose. In addition, complaints of various kinds would not recur. The pose resembles a wheel so it is called chakra (wheel) pose.

Chakrasana (Wheel Pose)

Procedure

Chakrasana (Wheel Pose)

- Lie on your back.
- Fold your legs and bring them to the buttocks.
- Place your hands parallel to the head. Now try to lift your body with your hands.
- Try to raise your back and buttocks in such a way so that the whole body looks like a wheel.
- Follow this with shavasana or the rest pose.
- A pose which has an opposite effect on the backbone, namely the paschimottanasana is recommended or, otherwise the practitioner will develop a back pain.

This pose is the most toughest, strenuous and wearisome. Indeed, it is a highly exhaustive pose. Many students have to take to rest immediately after performing it. Some even cannot lift up their bodies. Female students are mostly weaker than male ones in this case. Men and women whose waists are abnormally heavier than others and women wishing to get rid of their potbelly or waist should try this pose.

In fact, the beginners having dangerous physical complaints should start yoga on an absolutely empty stomach.

Diet

Having vegetable juices with ginger is helpful. Half-boiled dry fruits mixed with milk is the best food. Spicy and pungent food should be completely avoided. All those especially above 60 years should not take fried and fatty food at night. Foods containing starch especially rice, lentils could be taken sparingly – once a week only occasionally.

Care and Caution

The pose should not be tried without somebody's assistance in the beginning specially or it should be done carefully. It is imperative to perform the bow pose before doing the wheel pose. Bow pose prepares the ground for the wheel pose.

Home Remedies

- Fenugreek seeds or fenugreek roots or wheat saplings, grams, etc. have a rejuvenating power.
- The roots or the germinated seeds of the said plants and grams should be used raw with a little ginger, honey and a pinch of black pepper powder. No other food or drink in the world is so balanced as the cow's milk.
- Wheat saplings crushed and mixed with honey and a pinch of black pepper should be taken on an empty stomach.
- Dry fruits, carrots, grapes, almonds, etc. should be taken keeping an eye to one's digestive power. Milk, mango and bread (brown bread) provide a lot of energy.

Senility

Other Helpful Poses

- Tapotment – beating of all parts of the body from crown to the toes of the legs.
- Rolling (after having a glass of tepid water). If the stomach is windy, mix a pinch of rock salt in one or two glasses of water. Roll as many times as you feel like fast and not slowly. Roll both on the right and left sides.
- Cycling and anti-cycling many times.
- Paschimottanasana
- Bow pose
- Squatting
- Half peacock pose (Just press your navel with your elbows by facing the ground without lifting the legs but by keeping them straight.
- Cow mouth pose
- Head stand
- Meditation

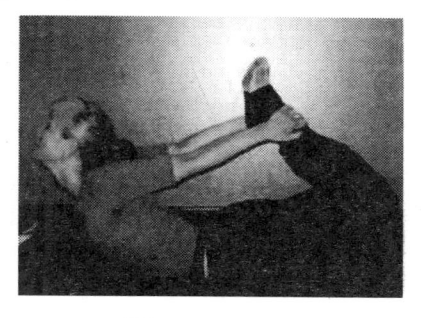

Dhanurasana (Bow Pose)

19. Dizziness

Vertigo or dizziness is caused mostly by a negative wind formed in the stomach. The negative wind makes its way up to the brain. Vertigo is also caused by a weak heart. It is not true that the pose under discussion will cure the complaint permanently unless adequate diet and proper homoeopathic and/or Ayurvedic remedies are taken.

Anaemia could also be a reason for dizziness or vertigo. Practising yoga asanas is absolutely useless if one wants to improve the condition overnight. The patient should pay attention to heart, stomach and lung problems mostly and necessary asanas namely, dog forward backward, sitting standing, peacock pose, wheel pose, cow mouth pose, headstand pose, etc. for a long period of time. Uttanmandukasana which resembles almost a fish pose should also be followed. It is better to have vegetarian food except fresh living fish which is really very much hygienic. Fish has a tendency to create constipation. Use sufficient fruits, green vegetables to guard against it. Because the complaint is caused by a kind of distorted wind. Ayurvedic medicines would help in curing this problem. Accompanied with it, yoga will cure the problem permanently.

Rest Pose would help in the acute condition. Rest pose with sprinkling of cold water in the eyes may be beneficial for the time-being. Wet bandage in the head for the time being may also be tried.

Uttanmandukasana

Uttanmandukasana is a very useful pose for dizziness. In addition to dizziness, this pose corrects the navel displacement too. This pose is also helpful in curing lung infections to a great deal.

Dizziness

Uttanmandukasana

Procedure

- Kneel down.
- Stretch out your feet parallel to the ground.
- Slowly sit on your feet and taking the help of your hands keep bending backwards slowly trying to touch the ground.
- Keep the chest towards the sky while putting the hands on the knees or back.

Variation Pose

Perform this asana in the lotus pose and not by sitting on the folded legs. The results are almost same. These poses are equally beneficial to women who derive better or more results from the fish pose.

Caution

While bending backwards try to make your cranium (back part of the head) touch the ground rather than the crown as it is very delicate.

Home Remedies

- The remedies that are connected with heart and stomach are applicable to dizziness also. The poses mentioned for headache which have been given before in this book would work wonders for dizziness.
- When one feels dizzy, lemon juice with a pinch of sugar can be really helpful.
- To keep the blood pressure under control lemon juice should be taken several times a day.
- Grapes are good for heart patients. Sun salutation (Dog forward and sitting standing) should be increased gradually. People suffering from low blood pressure or any heart problem should try this pose only in acute conditions.

Follow sun salutation for a longer period of time. Patients performing the sun salutation should not be reckless enjoyers of sexual pleasures but should maintain celibacy or else, the result of the head stand pose may be adverse in proportion to waywardness.

20. Chronic Constipation

Remedial Yoga Poses
1. Rolling
   - Lie on the back.
   - Fold your legs so that the heels touch the buttocks.
   - Embrace your legs with both arms.
   - It is better to have a glass of warm water before starting this. Now, roll on either side of the yoga seat about 7 to 8 times. The seat should be spacious enough. Go on rolling for about six or seven times first on the right hand side and, then on the left. Roll a little more forcefully so that the warm water if taken before starting this pose works nicely.

   Rolling

2. Sitting standing
3. Locust pose
4. Wheel pose
5. Peacock pose

6. Matsyendra pose
7. Scorpion pose
8. Head stand pose

Ayurvedic medicines and homoeopathic remedies work effectively in accompaniment to the asanas.

Diet

- Vegetables or vegetable juices, a lot of fresh fruits. Drumstick, stems of pumpkins should be consumed more.
- Wheat bran, scanned and then, mixed with vegetables or bread, broken wheat or milk etc are useful in fighting constipation – the cause of many diseases.

Dog forward-backward, useful in this case, produces a strong appetite.

Home Remedies

- A combination of honey, hot water and lemon also cures the complaint.
- Drinking hot water before bed at night is helpful. Some vegetables are highly useful for constipation, e.g. jackfruit, papaya (it is used both as a fruit and a vegetable). Ripe papaya is used as a fruit and the green one is used as a vegetable.
- Among the fruits, mango is known for removing constipation, cucumber is another produce. Mango helps in the formation of blood in the body. Mango is called nectar in Ayurveda.
- Wheat bran is also highly useful. Five teaspoonfuls of wheat bran in each meal should be taken twice a day but an excessive quantity brings forth negative wind and repeated visits to the toilet.
- The wheat bran should be scanned a few times with a strainer. The scanned wheat bran should be used. The

Chronic Constipation

scanned wheat bran can also be fried with a little clarified butter or ghee.

- Skipping is another way to fight constipation. Both male and female practitioner should skip in the morning and evening for about 15 minutes minimum after having a glass of tepid water. Skipping is also useful for maintaining the health of the entire stomach – which is responsible for most of the health problems. Hot, Bel, an Indian or Asian fruit, if green, may be taken by boiling it or ripe bel may also be eaten on an empty stomach to fight constipation.
- Keep two glasses of water in a pot made of copper for more than 12 hours. Early in the morning, drink it before going to toilet, it works.
- Either the juice of fenugreek leaves or having cooked fenugreek leaves is helpful in relieving constipation.

21. Sciatica

Sciatica, joint pain, arthritic problems – are all born out of distorted wind. The wind becomes excessive every day due to discontinuation of physical labour or yoga, making its dwelling house in the human economy. It may even be distorted to the extent of causing spondilitis, paralysis, which can affect the normal functioning of the brain.

Cycling

Procedure

- Lie down on your back.
- Lift your head about six inches above the ground. Repose your hands on both the sides of your thighs. Now move your legs forward as fast as you can in the same way as you ride a bicycle. Try doing the same procedure in the reverse direction which is anticycling. You should continue cycling till you get tired and your legs start paining.

Cycling

- This will increase your stamina day-by-day. It is also helpful to stabilise your lotus pose for a longer period (half

Sciatica

an hour minimum). when the legs are cycling, the doer should lift up his head about six inches above the ground and the two hands should repose at the sideways of the thighs. Eyes should be kept closed.

Benefits

- Mitigates pain in the groin.
- Partial remedy against waist pain, sciatica, etc.
- Increases the power to walk faster and for a longer period of time.

In order to remove excess water from the body which is the most visible reason for pain, etc, the patient should fast on water (boiled water preferably) for at least 24 hours for at least 10 days and on the eleventh day of both the new moon and full moon every month. This practice is followed by many spiritualists of India.

Remedies

- Two glasses of tepid water after meals every day works to a great extent. The water should be mixed with Triphala and abstemiousness should be observed in the night food.
- Avoid eating anything after sunset.
- A moderate quantity of garlic, however, is also useful.

Diet

- Foods containing starch should be used sparingly, e.g. rice, dal (lentils), sour foods, curd. Dry fruits are the best dietetic items for arthritic problems.

More Recommended Asanas

- Dog forward and backward (also called Sun salutations). In fact, this should be done until the doer sweats heavily. The patients of the age group of 25-45 should perform this 70 times or even more.

Speaking of Curing Diseases through Yoga

- Sitting standing, should be done double the number of dog forward – This is the general rule.
- Locust pose
- Peacock pose
- Expansion of legs
- Mahamudra
- Paschimottanasana
- Head stand

The patients should follow the sequence of posture remedies mentioned in this book under the guidance of a demonstrator because certain poses are prohibited to some students for some reasons.

Knee Stand Pose (Lotus Balance Pose)

Knee stand pose is also a highly effective pose for knee and joint pains.

Procedure

- Sit down and put one feet on the thigh of other leg and vice versa.
- Now lift your body and balance on your knees. Try to maintain the balance and stay. The pose looks like a mountain if the hands are lifted up. Some therefore call it mountain pose.

Lotus pose, expansion of legs, etc are other great remedies if maintained for about 15 minutes at a stretch.

Knee Stand Pose (Lotus Balance Pose)

# 22. Backache

Locust Pose

Locust is a kind of an insect which moves together in millions and destroys the crops. It has its posterior elevated.

Procedure

- Lie on your chest.
- Set your hands at the sides of the thighs and not on the thighs.

Preparatory Locust Pose

- Try to lift your one leg in the beginning and gradually start lifting up the other leg also.
- Lift up your legs as high as possible so that they make an angle of about sixty degrees (60°) from the ground.

Use the support of your palms and hands in the beginning. Try to perform this pose without the support of your hands only after some days.

Benefits

- Removes constipation.
- Eliminates backache.
- Corrects intestinal disorders, defects, namely displaced navel.
- Corrects the economy in a subtle way.

Other Recommended Asanas

- Paschimottanasana
- Camel pose
- Veepreet Karani Moodra
- Shoulder Stand
- Plough Pose
- Fish Pose
- Wheel pose
- Tree pose
- Narishodhanasana
- Trikonasana
- Hare pose

Veepareet Karani Mudra

Home Remedies

- Heat therapy as explained earlier (Burn down a quantity of wooden fuel, strain it and then bandage the affected area with this all night).
- Ayurvedic massaging oil, garlic oil or any other such oil.
- The spot if tied or bandaged with a layer of cotton all the night may be effective to some extent.
- Fomenting the affected area with a pillow which has been kept for hours in the sun.
- Fomentation with rice poultice.

Shoulder Stand

23. Health Care System

The human economy is bestowed by the blessings of Gods and the pervading agents in different parts of the body through different ways and means. The negative aspect of the human characters is dominated by the fair and bad elements of character: Tamas and Rajas – (a) material desire, (b) the ghosts dwelling inside our bodies are invisible agents who govern these tamas and rajas gunas, while the traits of different good virtues of a human character are under the command of Gods or Devas, or in other words, the power of the Satvic elements of man. Honesty, tenaciousness (for a good purpose), humanitarianism, modesty, manliness for a good cause, righteousness, etc. belong to the Devas or Gods. These Gods are departmental heads in consideration of this visible existence, namely, God of fire, water, earth, patience, etc.

Among all these Gods who govern the human economy according to the Karma-good or bad done by the children of the Supreme God, Sun God tops all the gods. The place or seat of the most powerful God – the sun God is situated at the navel part of the body (manipur chakra). Varuna, to cite another example, is the God of taste. So, he is pervaded in the tongue of human beings.

No one is sure of, speaking from the angle of a gross consciousness, how many miles away the Sun God has his asana (seat), how much is His temperature. The scientists till this day have only a hypothecation but actual distance, temperature, at sun, etc. are still a mystery. This is why Yogis worship the Sun God unlike the atheist scientists who microscope the Sun God as a huge glowing ball of fire or a planet.

Speaking of Curing Diseases through Yoga

Sun is the source of all energy. To worship the Sun God is to awaken the Manipur Chakra (the Navel) of the worshipper. If the navel part of the body could be stirred perfectly, the Sun God would destroy all kinds of diseases and will definitely awaken the Kundalini. The source of procreation is at the navel.The process of rousing the Manipur is what is called Dog forward and backward. It is interesting to know that dogs follow this posture. Sunsalutation has different postures but dog forward is the way that obviates the need to follow all the 12 or 16 varieties of sun salutations.

Research and practices have revealed the fact that only one particular way – the dog forward and backward – covers all the poses of sun salutations mentioned in the old books. It therefore saves time – the most valuable of a man's life. Dog forward depends upon age. Young people between the age group 25 to 45 should do this about 70-75 times. If tired, do shavasana and again do it and, thus, gradually increase the number. The number may be decreased according to aging; for old people – not many (15/20 times).

Whereas the rituals are, in most cases verbal, if not superficial, the Dog forward pose is perfectly practical. The result of this exercise is obtainable immediately. The posture increases muscle power, it makes the appearance muscular, hence, some female stay away from doing this pose. But, however, female students too should do this pose not so many times but ten times maximum. The pose is not needed to be done twice a day; only once especially on an empty stomach is enough. Dand is another name of this pose in Hindi.

The Persian devotees have the Sun as their only Deity. Shamboo, the son of the Lord Krishna, was attacked with leprosy. As the mythology goes, not even the God of Medicine, Ashwinee, succeeded in curing Shamboo. Lord Krishna, then, prostrated unto the Sun, whose mystery science will never succeed to decipher, touched Shambo, bestowed blessings on him. Shamboo practised this pose and was cured absolutely.

Health Care System

Blessings of the Sun God

(1) It corrects the malformation of the physical structure, expands chest and in accompaniment with the sitting standing posture it makes the body look physically more perfect. Expanded chest is a beauty both for men and women. The waist becomes attractively proportionate to the chest. Expanded chest is prophylactic as it draws more oxygen. Asphyxia could well be fought with this remedy.

(2) Manliness or he-manship is unfolded day-by-day. Dispirited souls become vivacious in a shortest period of practice. The countenance becomes bright, glazy or shining. All the visible and invisible blood-circulating passages are so intensely toned up that this pose could well be termed as the greatest internal masseur.

(3) It makes the spinal cord flexible gradually.

(4) It is reported by some students that it increases appetite because it backs up the function of the pancreas. Many pupils of stomach diseases have heaved a sigh of relief by this particular pose only.

(5) One of the greatest boon of this pose is that it fights skin diseases. Paschimottan pose or tree pose, is also another remedy against skin diseases, because it purifies blood by almost grinding the foodstuff whatsoever falls into the pancreas.

(6) Lungs become more potent day-by-day.

(7) It uproots insomnia, nightmare and nocturnal nuisance very effectively. The yogis enjoy sound sleep, however they don't sleep for long hours.

(8) Work and not idleness is another boon. The practitioner practises more vigorously than before. When he walks, his legs move like flying birds.

(9) Sun salutation (Surya Namaskar) corrects the gait of the doer. There are men and women who walk in an ugly way. When the practitioner enjoys this pose, his chest being

broad, the feet moves faster than before, as if someone is pushing him from his back.

(10) Flaccidity, obesity and flabbiness have no room in the human body any more.

To name a few, the following problems of stomach and related diseases like are uprooted forever giving new lease of life to the patient. Halitosis, toothache, gastritis, dyspepsia, vertigo, headache, hernia, stomach worms, pruritus (itching of anus) liver diseases, appendicitis, etc.

Halitosis can be cured if the stomach is free from undigested food. Halitosis is a premonition of other diseases, it undermines the personality of the patient when he comes in contact with his acquainted persons. Halitosis is mainly caused by improper digestion of food.

Remedies Against Halitosis

- Take some fenugreek seeds, boil them for sometime, strain and drink it – This would help to solve bad breath.
- Boil one or two cardamoms crushed for some time; strain it, mix it with water in which some rose petals of were put for about 12 hours. Mix both the waters and drink it. This is also a great help. Cleanliness of stomach through proper digestion is the permanent cure.

Do's and Don'ts

(1) Scriptures are not unanimous in its opinions as to when the pregnant women should stop doing this pose (sun salutation). However, it is better to stop this pose as soon as the female conceives.

(2) The practice should not be intensified hastily.

(3) Try to look at the sky as you finish the pose each time.

(4) Head between the Legs Pose should be done for a sufficient number of times in proportion to this pose or, otherwise you may have a backache.

Health Care System

(5) Keep your mouth, eyes and anus closed while you practise.
(6) Beware of sexual excitement (especially young practitioners).

Surya Namaskar (Sun Salutation)

Procedure

- Facing the east join your palms, set them to your chest and pray to the Sun god.
- Bend forward and place your palms on the ground by maintaining some distance between your feet.
- Thus, the backbone should look as an apex of a triangle.
- Now, push back your body, as a preparatory step to make a nose drive into the ground. Nose drive is a word which is used by fighter pilots.
- The nose drive being reached, lift up your head to look at the sky by fixing your palms at the same place you had kept at the start.
- Again start with step 4 (i.e. push back) and repeat. Until you gasp and sweat heavily, go on and on. When you push back each time, give a preparatory jerk to your lower part so that the exercise can be done with a full physical force.
- If need be, follow rest pose.
- Repeat this.

Diet

- Eat less, or eat in moderation. Eat more vegetables preferably their juice.
- Dry fruits and nuts, etc. should be taken sparingly, keeping an eye to night pollution.
- Stop eating at irregular intervals. Masticate 15-20 times each mouthful of food.

24. Knee Joint Problems

Sitting and standing is best to alleviate joint pain. This is purely a physical posture but it helps a lot to pave the way for some other poses, namely expansion of legs, lotus pose, cow mouth pose, paschimottan pose, kandapeerasana (also named by the author as Liberation pose), etc. Sitting standing should be done twice the number of dog forward to maintain the optimum proportionality of the chest and lower part of the body. If this rule is not observed, then there may be a malformation – the chest can get too much expanded and the waist narrow.

Sitting and Standing

Patients whose legs fidget will be highly benefited. To squat and stand up without the help of any support is better. A glass of tepid water mixed with a spoonful of black salt, if taken before doing this pose may help the doer to evacuate both the accumulated stool and downward unhygienic wind.

Other Helpful Poses
- Paschimottanasana
- Camel pose

Knee Joint Problems

- Veepareet karani mudra
- Shoulder stand
- Plough pose
- Fish pose
- Peacock pose
- Matsyendra pose
- Yoga mudra
- Head stand
- Rest pose
- Agnisar dhauti
- Rest pose

Squatting

Agni Sar Dhauti

- Sit preferably in the Lotus pose.
- Catch the sides of your waist with your thumbs.
- Thrust or press the navel with the fingers of the hands slowly and then violently, many times, 100 times or more than that.
- Keep looking in front.
- Before doing this pose have a glass of water. Some students prefer rolling after it for constipation, etc. This should be done on an empty stomach. It can also be done after five hours of taking a meal.

25. Body Pain

Massage

- Sit down and fold one of your legs and bring it close to the buttocks.
- Start pressing your body starting from the crown of the head to the toes repeatedly. This is the first way of massaging.
- Tapotment – Beating all the parts of your body, not very gently.
- The third way of massaging is with the help of herbal or ayurvedic oils.

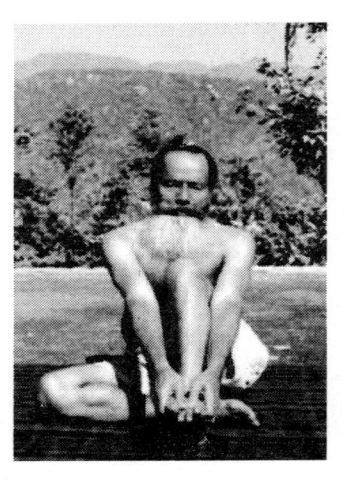

Massaging

Diet

- Fasting with only boiled water approximately 4 its in 24 hours is the best means. Stop eating foods which contain starch in them.
- Try to have more of dry fruits, beans, vegetables, broken wheat, etc.

Massaging with any body oil (herbal, ayurvedic, etc.) works moderately but not permanently. To cure the complaint permanently, regular practice of Yoga with an observance of dietetic rules is the best way.

Body Pain

Home Remedies

- Castor oil should be mixed with a reasonable quantity of garlic and heated with a moderate temperature and then strained. This can be used for massaging.
- Hot milk mixed with garlic and a pinch of black salt can be taken. But be cautious of using it, if you have piles, as it may cause bleeding.
- Homoeopathic remedies are also very useful, namely oxalic acid – 200 (three drops with a dropper early in the morning or before going to bed).
- If the body, knee, hands, pain on account of doing asanas, Arnica – 30 is the remedy. Arnica 200 may be taken if the complaint is as old as a minimum of one year.
- The patient should take bath in hot or cold water with common salt or sea salt mixed in it.
- Fasting is another great measure.
- Sponge bed is unhygienic. Use cotton-made mattress.
- Relax in the sun till you start sweating. The head should be covered to protect the heat of the sun.
- Hare pose is also highly effective.
- Massage the body with any of the following oils or all of them mixed together – mustard oil, tarpin oil, garlic oil, mint oil and garlic oil. Garlic oil should be used in less quantity.
- Foods which have a cooling effect like ice cream, sour foods are not congenial but harmful.
- Usage of garlic in the dish should be increased.
- Ayurvedic massaging oils work satisfactorily but only for some time. The best process is to become a regular practitioner of Yoga, the best blessings of the God.

Tapotment

26. Stomach Problems

Bhujangasana (Snake Pose)

Procedure
- Lie down on your chest.
- Place both your hands parallel to your chest.
- Now try to lift your head, chest and waist from the ground taking the support from your arms.

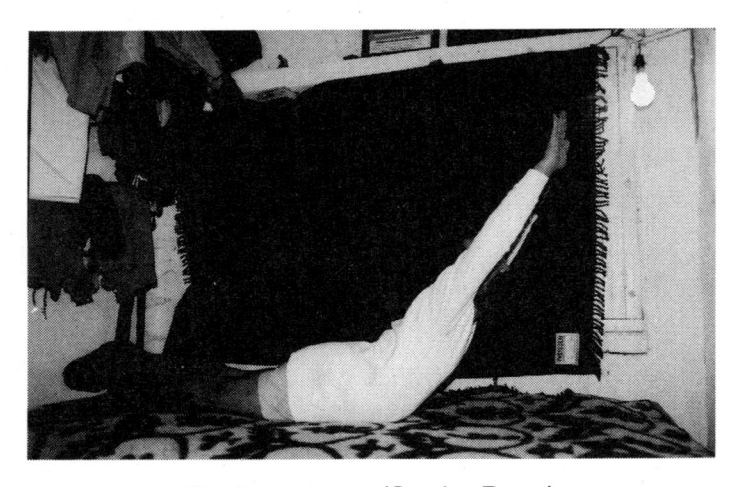

Bhujangasana (Snake Pose)

There is another way of doing this asana. Instead of keeping your hands parallel to your chest and taking support of your hands to lift your body up, keep your arms straight. Now try to raise your

Stomach Problems

body without any support as snakes do not have hands or legs. This pose looks like a snake so it is also called snake pose.

Recommended Yoga Poses
- Dog forward and backward
- Sittingstanding (squatting) should be double the Dog forward
- Peacock pose (special attention)
- Matsyendra pose and a few more in consultation with a teacher or guru.
- Narishodhasana
- Scorpion pose
- Lastly, snake pose is a highly useful.

Benefits

Stomach complaints, wind, indigestion, distension, etc. can be cured by this asana.

Caution

It is better to perform locust pose after this pose. The patients of Hernia or Orchitis (inflammation of the testicles) should pay attention to the state of their complaints which can get aggravated by the locust pose in some cases.

Home Remedies
- A combination of ginger juice, black pepper and rock salt can be taken before going to bed.
- Grind some cumin seeds, add black pepper, rock salt and ginger to it. Eat this with lemon juice for about a week (thrice a day).
- Lemon mixed with water protects vomiting also.

- A combination of lemon, water and black pepper is effective in liver diseases also.
- Apple is highly useful. Green apple is more useful.

Do's and Don'ts

- The patient should vomit (by inserting his fingers into the throat) after about five hours of eating a meal whenever he feels uneasy. It can also be done every day if the patient wants. This will help the stomach get rid of the toxins.
- Don't eat to your fullest. Always eat less than your hunger.
- Eating outside or having fast food is not healthy.
- The patient should include a sufficient quantity of radish, ginger, lemon juice and rock salt in his food every day.
- Foul smell from the mouth (halitosis) is a produce of stomach disorders in most cases. However, in addition to fenugreek juice, gargling with mint juice also does wonders.
- Melon is a useful fruit to destroy acidity, gastritis, inflammation, etc. Like melon, sweet lemon is also good for acidity.
- Fig is a good fruit for constipation and a bad liver. Fig when used in milk, works as a good laxative too.
- Have more of fresh salads.
- Avoid meat as much as possible. Meat coagulates wind in different nook and corner of the body and hence makes the eater incapacitate to bend bodies and do yoga. Meat is an acid food. But, fresh fish (a river or sea) is good for eyes as well as for the whole body. Fast once in 10 days. During fasting live only on water, preferably boiled water.

27. Development of Personality

The word personality is always used in a lofty sense in the same way as the word 'meditation' is used in the kingdom of God only and for no other objects, men or matter.

Personality is a bundle of virtues with the help of which an individual represents himself. Among the creatures, which have been created by the Creator or Nature in the eyes of the atheists, man is the last produce of the Creator. The same dogma is presented by the biologists who claim that monkeys are the last ancestors of human beings. Although there are opinions in this regard. The scriptures concluded that God became satisfied only after creating human beings as the last step by reason of the fact that it is man who can realise what he is. Animals have no right to attain realisation on account of the anatomical reason that they cannot sit erect or their backbone can never stay perpendicular to the ground. Backbone should be perpendicular to the ground – a fact which rouses the Kundalini whether some spiritualists realise this through Bhakti, Karma or Hatha system of ontology.

Yoga of Asanas is the most dependable way to improve your personality day by day.

Gorakhasana

Gorakhasana

Gorakshanathji, a great spiritual king, a great Yogi, disciple of a marvellous Yogi named Shri Shri Matsyendranathji, used to perform this pose for a long period of time. This pose has, therefore been named after Sri Sri Gorakhnathji.

In fact, this is a pose for meditation and therefore, can be done even after sheershasana (headstand). The pose is beautiful to look at if it can be done in a perfect way.

Procedure

- Sit erect.
- Fold your legs keeping one leg on the thigh of the other.
- Now with the help of your hands lift your legs and your body from the ground.
- When you fold your legs a gap will get created in between them. Swing forward and backward with the object of sitting on the said gap. Try to improve the swinging day-by-day. You are sure to sit on the destined gap within a week or so.
- The anus, bear in mind it, should be just in the middle of the gap only then the pose would work completely. According to *Bhagwad Gita* – 'He whose vital force reaches the central spot lying between the brows, at the time of death, who remembers Me with devotion and Yoga Kriyas (actions) is liberated'. Sincere Yoga practitioners feel this intuitive knowledge on many occasions during the practice of this pose.

One can easily improve the staying time of this pose by reading a book while sitting in this posture. The time should be increased each day slowly. The performance can achieve optimum psycho physiological as well as spiritual benefits by practising Japa (counting the rosary, preferably in the right hand and the left hand to be used for counting the number of rounds only). Japa, therefore is another greatest practical way of practising this pose.

Benefits

- As for therapeutic benefits, when mool bandh is maintained very nicely, the anus being heated, passes out unwanted and unhygienic wind from the stomach, prohibits irregular supply of blood to the centre of the rectum.
- Anal diseases, namely, piles, pruritus annie (itching of anus etc.) are highly protected although in running conditions of diseases, it is unwise to depend on Yoga and asanas – which is prophylactic and curative if the dietetic regulations are maintained satisfactorily. Yoga of asanas prepares the ground to restore health in course of time. The period depends mainly on intensity of the disease, dietetic rules, etc. but it is guaranteed that yoga has spiritual value.
- Concentration of mind is the greatest boon of this pose on condition that the doer has a spirit of renouncing the material world.
- This pose has its effect on the urinary system of the human physiology. Therefore, it works a lot for the health of the urinary system. Inabilities to retain urine, inflammation. are highly safeguarded by this pose.
- Abdominal parts of the body are nicely repaired, reconstructed in the right way, if done for a considerable period of time.

Once Swami Vivekananda, the monk who had stirred the sentiment of the United States of America by dint of his incendiary oratorical excellence in religion – was absorbed in studying a book. One of his disciples kept waiting for him. More than an hour passed out, Swami kept glued to the book. Later on when he finished reading the book he thanked his disciple for her extraordinary patience and sense of reverence.

Swami Vivekananda

The more the sushumna canal (central subtle passage) of the backbone is free from filthy substances namely, obesity, wind, etc. the more is the concentration of the practitioner would be.

The following poses have been recommended for the development of personality:
- Success pose or siddhasana
- Half cow mouth pose
- Lotus pose
- Expansion of legs
- Gorakhasana
- Ordinary pose

28. Lung Diseases

Gomukhasana (Cow mouth pose front side)

This is called cow mouth pose as the two thighs look exactly like the mouth of a cow. In Sanskrit '*Gow*' means cow, and '*Mukh*', mouth.

Procedure

- Sit down and fold your left leg.
- Take the right leg over the left in the opposite direction so that the two folded legs resemble a 'V'.
- Sit on the heels.
- Now raise the right hand and take it towards your back. Take the left hand also towards the back and try to interlock the fingers of both the hands.
- Not to speak of the instruction repeatedly, the anus should be kept closed. Keep your eyes also closed.
- Repeat the pose with the other leg also.

In the half cow mouth pose the only difference is that the hands rest on the knees.

Benefits

- As per the ancient scriptures of our forefathers, this pose is highly useful for meditation perhaps, only next to siddhasana (success pose). Some books prefer even this pose to the success pose. However, it is a matter of intuitive knowledge only. The spiritual value of this pose is immense.

Speaking of Curing Diseases through Yoga

- This pose keeps a check on sexual excitement.
- It relieves knee pain to some extent.
- Lung complaints are highly repaired with this pose because when this pose is done by interlocking the fingers at the back, one lung is pressed, the other is unaffected. The result being that the doer inhales more air (oxygen) and then, when hands are changed, the same process is repeated.
- People suffering from angina pectoris (pain in the chest), tuberculosis, accumulation of excessive nicotine in the lungs by smoking a lot, respiratory troubles (asthmatic diseases) bronchitis, etc. are advised to do this pose for about 15 minutes.
- Other recommended poses are: scorpion pose, wheel pose, tree pose, peacock pose, shoulder stand, veepareet karani mudra, fish pose, etc.

Diet

- The diet should be a little pungent, irritating and stirring – ginger, black pepper, garlic, honey, fish, egg (not meat) cabbage, etc. are good. Artificially produced eggs are not very effective.
- All kinds of medicinal remedies should be adopted simultaneously, if possible, to hold the complaint in check and, then a vigorous exercise of Yoga should be done.
- However, people suffering from respiratory diseases, heart diseases, blood pressure, bronchial disorders should drink a mixture of the following home-made ingredients. Half a glass of hot water, with one lemon squeezed in to it and a tablespoon of ginger (newly harvested especially), three teaspoonfuls of honey, four or five grains of black pepper – may be taken thrice or more in an acute condition but twice in a normal one.

Lung Diseases

- In case of a bout of cough, a mixture of sugar, black pepper, rock salt should be sucked with lemon juice. But this is a temporary remedy.

Padmasana or Lotus Pose

Padma means lotus and hence the name padmasana or the lotus pose. Lotus pose is used both for breathing exercises and for meditation. When the undersurface of the feet is set on the thighs nicely, the soles look like petals of a flower. The navel of a human being has been compared to lotus by many scriptures on many occasions. Thus, the navel resembles a lotus, the petals of which are upturned. Since the soles have a bright, reddish colour, the naming of the pose is highly reasonable.

Procedure

- Sit erect.
- Fold your left leg and place it on the thigh of the right leg. Set the heel a little below the navel and at a distance of about three inches from the navel.
- Do the same with the other leg too. Thus, the two heels would be set at almost an equal distance from the navel. Keep your back straight. Bent the head forward slightly.
- There is a sudden jerk as if the meditator would fall back.
- There is a severe shaking and jerking (flesh creeping) effect with or without the vision of any God, ghost or apparitions.
- The feeling is so intense that the touch of any dearest one also – wife, mother husband, etc. is dislikable – "Bazya Sparsheshu Asakta Atma Vindati Atmani Yat Suksham"– *Bhagwad Gita.*
- The body gets heated up and the seat on which the Yogi sits becomes as hot as fire.

Sri Sri Ramkrishna observes, "For three days there was no feeling of any senses." His body was covered with wet blankets to recover from the too much heat of the body. According to His Holiness "There is no knowledge without the rise of the Kundalini."

Sri Ramkrishna Paramahansa

Benefits

- The pose if done for a long time evacuates excessive or unwanted wind in the stomach. Sometimes it removes constipation (especially if one glass of tepid water is consumed before doing this pose).
- It helps in improving concentration because the wind becomes normal.
- Knee problems are also overcomed by this asana.
- The most striking and perceptible usefulness of this pose is observed in the fact that the mind becomes stable, balanced and restful in a short period of time (if M.B. is followed and not forgot).
- Padmasana (Lotus pose) is used mostly for breathing exercises and meditation. The two sides of navel being pressed nicely by the two heels and the mool bandh is followed.
- The doer starts feeling a mood of introversion, because the Kundalini area is warmed up. It is only for this reason Gods like Shiva and other sages are found sitting in this pose in their various pictures.

Lung Diseases

- To meditate in this pose, it is wise to use a cushion which should be as thick as four inches. A cushion will help to irritate the navel part thereby stirring the Kundalini – the dormant and invisible power in a meditator's body.

The symptoms of the Kundalini Mother being awakened are many. A few are being given so that the rising Yogins can tally with their intuitive experiences and can enjoy them thoroughly: Jerking, light etc.

Expansion of Legs

Expansion of legs is another good process of meditation by the most important reason of the fact that the vital force of both male and female meditators starts accumulating near the sushumna and, then, starts rising up by thrusting itself upwards provided the meditator practises celibacy. The spiritual boon of this posture is a rigid penance, no doubt. When the two legs are stretched out by making them parallel to the anus, the hamstring pains. The legs are tightened in the same way as the strings of a sitar. The hands could be put on the heels, on the lap or a prayer posture could be maintained. But the back should be absolutely straight except a slight bend towards the front so that a tribundh could be maintained although it happens naturally. Mool bandh must be followed without mistake. Deep concentration in this pose is a verified experiment of hundreds of students. The doer should try to set the feet parallel to the anus slowly every day. To make it a success, he should place one hand behind the back and the other at the front and advance slowly every day with patience.

Expansion of Legs

Benefit

- Relief from joint pains, sciatica, etc.
- Reduction of excessive flesh both in thighs and in the posterior.
- Correction of respiratory disproportion – some people inhale more and exhale less or vice versa.
- Flexibility of waist.
- Sexual excitement comes to a grinding halt certainly.
- Functioning of brain improves.

Gorakhasana is also a useful pose for lung diseases.

Gorakhasana

29. Diabetes

Diabetes is the name of a disease in which sugar and starch are not assimilated in the human economy and, hence, the undigested left outs produce various kinds of problems. Frequent urination, other urinary complaints, skin diseases, loss of reproductive power – are some of the produces of this complaint.

Here there is a physiological process called matsyendrasana pose, which has been found to be highly remedial to fight this complaint. A large number of victims have reported positive results after practising this pose.

Matsyendrasana (Preparatory Pose)

Procedure

- Sit on the ground with your back perfectly straight.
- Fold your right leg and bring it close to the anus.
- Keep the left leg folded and bring it close to the chest with the foot resting on the ground. Now take it over the right leg and place the left foot firmly on the ground.
- Now with your right hand try to catch hold of the left leg's big toe by trying to reach towards it from outside the left leg.

Preparatory Matsyendrasana

- Place the left hand on the ground behind the back by making sure that your head, chest and shoulders are all turned backwards.
- Maintain the stay without movement for sometime.
- Repeat the same process with the other leg too.

This pose is more advanced, covers half the usefulness of the full Matsyendra pose.

There is another way of doing this asana. This process is applicable to those who cannot bend their legs to the extent required. Stand near a log or a metal pipe whose tip is not hollow but solid, or, the tip should be plain, smooth but solid or, in other words it does not hurt your belly. Now hold it and slowly touch the tip of the pipe. Maintain the pressure, but most students discard it on the ground that it is a ludicrous way. But it really works.

Matsendrio Nathji, the great yogi acknowledged by one and all, did not discover this pose to get rid of diabetes but for attaining enlightenment which he fulfilled in His life. To be brief, Kundalini – the first step to Realisation is awakened when this pose is performed. 'Seek the kingdom of God, all other things would be added unto you'. This Biblical directive is fulfilled by the performance of this pose for a certain period of time.

Benefits
- First of all, it kills the intestinal or stomach worms – tape worm, ring worm, etc. which trouble the victim in so many ways – all of a sudden there would be a watery flow, a tendency to vomit, loose motion, vertigo, etc. All kinds of worms are destroyed by the blessings of this asana alone.
- Secondly, it corrects the pancreas as it helps to rouse the pancreas fire if done for a period to time. Gradually the time period of the asana should be increased if maximum results have to be obtained.

- Impaired digestive system can be corrected with the help of this pose. Liver function, stomach disorders, acidity, etc. are absolutely cured by it.
- Not to speak of diabetes, some other urinary complaints are also cured by this pose provided a strict observance of dietetic rules is observed.

Home Remedies

The diabetic should take curd early in the morning (after Yogasana). The curd should be mixed with water, rock salt and cumin seed powder. The cumin seeds should be fried and not raw. Papaya is a good fruit for diabetics.

Other Recommended Postures

- Shoulder stand, plough pose and fish pose should be done one after another.
- Fish pose is done half the total time consumed by the shoulder stand and plough poses. Veepareet karani mudra is done before the shoulder stand pose.
- Expansion of legs
- Gorakshasana
- Peacock pose
- Yoga mudra
- Lotus pose
- Bhunmanasana
- Sun salutation
- Sitting standing
- Head stand

According to Ayurvedic instructions, a few glasses of water should be taken before doing the pose so that the urinary bladder gets nicely emptied. Patients suffering from urinary disorders should avoid pungent spices in the food. Sunsalutation should be done many times especially at a stretch and abstain from sexual activities.

The process of utilising the Yoga Mudra for the purpose of fighting diabetes is as follows:-

Yog Mudra (Variation Pose)

Procedure

- Sit erect in the lotus pose, if not possible, in the ordinary pose.
- Make your hands into a fist and put them a little below the navel. Now try to touch your nose to the ground. While bending, follow exhalation, maintain the pose for sometime, say 15 minutes or so.
- Avoid starch food – rice, etc. Fish pose is also considered to be a great weapon to fight diabetes.

Ardhkoomarasana (Half-tortoise Pose)

Procedure

- Kneel down and sit on your legs.
- Press the navel with the elbows. Keep bending and continue looking forward.
- Maintain the pose for sometime.

Matsyendrasana and Karnapeerasana are the most effective postures.

Home Remedies for Urinary Complaints

- Eat vegetables with fig which is highly beneficial for urinary complaints. Fig is useful for problems related to menstruation too. Bitter gourd (Hairy – mordica, *Karela* in Hindi language), Jambul, tomatoes, coconut, spinach are good for this complaint.

Diabetes

- ... works better on an empty stomach.
- Bitter gourd juice mitigates urinary inflammations.
- A dust of Jambul (Indian name) seed with half a cup of plain water thrice a day is good for diabetic patients.
- Radish leaf and radish both are useful in overcoming the problem of retention of urine or inflammation. Milk mixed with cardamom is also helpful for the same purpose.
- Coconut oil, sugarcane juice, coriander juice are helpful remedies.
- Sugar candy is beneficial for urinary inflammation.

30. Piles

To fight piles, the foremost task is to keep the stomach clean and unconstipated. If you are already attacked, the best suggestion is to undergo a surgical operation and after the recovery, follow Yoga and strict dietetic rules which will ensure that no further attacks But in many cases it is experienced that the victim, for reasons whatsoever, paves the way for the disease mostly by dint of an unhygienic way of life. Unhealthy lifestyle, wrong eating habits are the main causes of the diseases. Like piles, some more complaints like hernia, etc. are also caused due to the above reasons.

Scorpion Pose

Scorpion Pose

Procedure

- Stand on the head or follow head stand pose.
- While maintaining the balance of the body stem slowly fold your legs and move them forward.
- The whole body should be lifted with the hands.
- Try to stay this pose and then relax.
- Now your physical appearance will resemble a scorpion and hence the name.

Piles

The Other Beneficial Postures

- Sun Salutations till the body starts sweating
- Sitting standing till the knees are unbearably painful.
- Locust pose
- Peacock pose
- Matsyendrasana
- Scorpion pose (In the picture page 106)
- Expansion of legs (special attention)
- Gorakhasana

Bhunamasana

After performing the expansion of legs, the doer should catch the toes of both the legs and try to touch his chest, mouth or chin on slowing the floor by and by. Perfection would be found only after days but not in a day or two. Please, be patient.

Other Benefits

Waist pain vanishes without any other remedies. For a waist pain, however, the locust pose is also a great remedy. Concentration of mind is a great boon because the respiration comes to a halt slowly. The patient should practise the special poses for piles for a longer period of time, say 15 minutes each pose.

Diet and Temporary Remedies

- Laxative medicinal remedies – Allopathic, Ayurvedic, or Homoeopathic remedies should be taken.
- When attacked, the best way is to use medicinal remedies and at the same time follow fasting on a liquid diet - fruit juices, vegetable juices or curd, etc.

- Bleeding can be checked with medicine if the stomach is not allowed to be constipated in any way. Therefore, liquid food along with medicines, fruit juices, etc. is the greatest remedies. If the patient is averse to fruit juices wheat bran can also be given.
- To fight constipation, go through the constipation poses again. When piles is in an acute state, if a lemon cut into two pieces is sucked with a pinch of rock salt it gives immediate relief.
- Trifala churan (churan means powder) an ayurvedic remedy is reported to be highly beneficial to combat this complaint. One or two spoonfuls each time, twice a day can be taken for general health.
- Non-vegetarian food should be avoided. The vegetables that produce wind should be prohibited.
- The soil therapy is also useful to fight piles. The place from where the soil is to be collected should be neat and clean, and free from pebbles or small stones. If the doctor is skillful, homoeopathic remedies work nicely.

Diet

- One should have more of fibrous foods and green vegetables to fight constipation.
- Avoid having foods which are too warm in nature, drinks and pungent spices. Restrain from smoking and stop the intake of alcoholic drinks completely.

31. Blood Pressure

Blood pressure, thrombosis, stroke, hernia, paralysis, spondilitis, arthritis, hemicrania, etc. are connected with the wrong run of wind in the human body. Most people, for reasons whatsoever, cannot maintain a healthy lifestyle to protect their health. Imperfect digestion, wrong eating habits create excessive wind in the stomach every day that can cause many problems.

Mayurasana (Peacock Pose)

Mayurasana (Peacock Pose)

Procedure

- Kneel down on the seat.
- Join your elbows in an upturned or reverse direction the small fingers of both the hands will now be parallel to each other. The other fingers should be adjacent to one another.
- Try to fold the elbows so that they touch your navel when you have touched the navel with the elbow try to lift up one leg so that the entire weight of your body is on the elbows only. After a few days try doing the asana with both the legs lifted up in the air your target should be lift up the legs as high as 45 degrees from the waist.
- The more you can stay in this position the better it is.

Speaking of Curing Diseases through Yoga

A yoga practitioner should visit his doctor regularly to undergo a health check-up and practise the yoga asanas regularly.

The following postures would also keep the blood pressure in control:

- Dead Pose – The usual way of maintaining the dead pose is to think on the blue firmament. The patient should take a glass of plain water mixed with lemon before doing this pose.
- Sun Salutation (till sweating profusely).
- Head stand (special attention)
- Cow mouth pose
- Squatting
- Naval exercise
- Mahamudra
- Tree pose
- Scorpion pose
- Hare pose
- Rest pose may well be called high blood pressure pose.

Blood pressure, thrombosis, heart disease, etc. as have been mentioned in this topic have only one remedy, i.e. Yoga. To beat the intensity, the patient can take the help of medicines for some days and then start yoga vigorously.

Live mainly on liquid foods – vegetable juices, fruit juices or milk, etc. especially during the night so that the morning programme of Yoga could be improved in a

Khagasana (Harepose)

Tree pose

Blood Pressure

short period of time. Gradually, all the complaints of the body will vanish. Fruits, vegetables etc.- the juice of which the patient takes should be in accordance with his complaints for which an ayurvedic doctor may be consulted.

Blood pressure is a condition of economy in which the blood is impeded by the accumulation of cholesterol in the arteries and veins.

Protective Home Remedies

- Raisins kept in water for hours eaten for a long time are said to be beneficial for low blood pressure.
- Carrot mixed with honey is good for low blood pressure.
- Red beat, a vegetable along with its leaves, if taken in the form juice is conducive for low blood pressure. Grape is a highly useful fruit for heart patients.
- Carrot is used for this disease in many ways – cooked, salad, pickles, etc. A mixture of ginger, cardamom and fenugreek (green) is useful for low blood pressure.
- Carrot jam is useful for high blood pressure too.
- Watermelon is prescribed by doctors to reduce weight, fat and obesity. It is an alkaline food.
- Chappati with milk is useful for high blood pressure. Its intake lowers down high blood pressure.
- The juice of coriander (dhania), lemon and sugar candy can beat down high blood pressure.
- The patient should follow rest pose or shavasana after taking this remedy. Rest pose is also helpful in an acute state.
- Having lemonade (one lemon for a glass) thrice or four times a day can keep the blood pressure in control.
- Wheat saplings (6 to 7 in inches in height) used in vegetables (not fruits) or crushed to juices are highly

beneficial for heart patients. Mentioned else where, a combination of gourd (Jukinee-*louki* in Hindi) and mint to be mixed with a reasonable quantity of ginger, dry or green and / or black pepper should be taken 4 times a day. This is reported to be highly useful for heart diseases. It should be taken for many days at a stretch. People suffering from heart problems should avoid non-vegetarian food and abstain from alcohol and smoking.

Ancient scriptures give evidence to specify certain postures meant for a special complaint too. Fish pose or Matsyasana is not done separately. It is done after the shoulder stand for the purpose of guarding against neck pain. There is a possibility of the neck being attacked by unequal distribution of wind, if this pose is not done immediately after the shoulder stand. The amount of time to be consumed by this pose should approximately be half the total time consumed by veepareet karani mudra, shoulder stand and plough pose. This is the traditional recommendation of the ancient scriptures.

Plough Pose

Plough Pose

Blood Pressure

Procedure

- Lie down on your back.
- Slowly lift your legs, waist with the help of your hands.
- Lift your whole body from the ground except your shoulders and head.
- Now slowly take your legs above your head in the opposite direction so that your feet touch the ground.
- Keep your hands on the ground only.

This pose looks like a plough hence its name.

When this pose is done, the doer should rotate his eye balls in different directions from right to left and from left to right. Backache is brought under control by doing this exercise.

All kinds of ovarian (structural) defects that could be responsible for barrenness could be brought to an orderly state. Thus, women should practise it for their own health. It is in fact, an invigorating posture for women.

32. Menstrual Problems

Fish Pose

Procedure

- Sit in the lotus pose (This is important for the lotus pose has a direct impact on the internal structure of the doer. In the half lotus pose, one leg is on the thigh of the other leg.)

Fish Pose

- Now lie on your back.
- Take your back and cranium to the floor.
- Hold the toes of both the feet with your fingers.
- Keep the elbows on the ground.
- The eyes could be kept closed or open in this pose as the result is the same.
- The chest should be lifted up considerably. Female students should bear in mind that they should not be too shy to perform this pose in the presence of male yoga teachers. The chest should be inflated to the fullest.

Menstrual Problems

Home Remedies

- For excessive discharge coriander, a spice daily used in cooking is highly beneficial. About 250 gms of coriander should be mixed in water and boiled till the water is reduced to one fourth of the quantity. Strain and drink it on an empty stomach especially. Use sugar-candy mixed with water after an hour without fail.
- Carrot seed should be mixed with treacle in case of irregular menstrual cycle. One and a half teaspoon of carrot seeds and five teaspoon of treacle is the proportion.
- If treacle is not found, molasses will do. About two teaspoon's of black cumin seed powder if taken with water (early morning especially) may induce menstruation.
- A few pieces of asafoetida may be used if the said powder causes a little pain in the stomach.

33. Pot Belly

Dhanurasana (Bow Pose)

Procedure

- Lie on your chest.
- Bend your legs backwards and try to hold your feet with your hands.
- Lift your head and take it back and try to look at the sky as far as possible while the legs should be pulled severely so that the entire weight of your body rests absolutely on your navel only. When exhausted, have rest in the crocodile pose which is as follows.

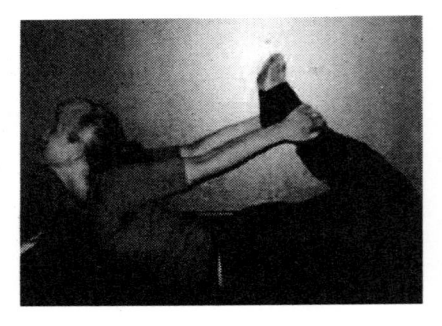

Dhanurasana (Bow Pose)

Crocodile Pose

Procedure

- Lie on your chest. Stretch out your legs, keep them apart maintaining a distance of about two and a half feet from each other.
- Keep the arms on the ground on both sides and relax. You will probably fall asleep.

Pot Belly

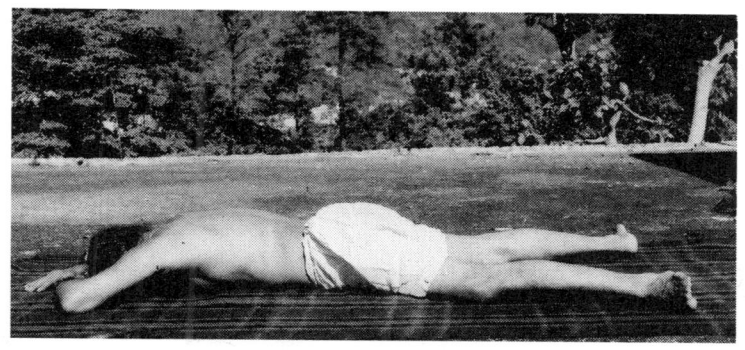

Makarasana (Crocodile Pose)

Although it is said that this pose is helpful for reducing a pot belly but experience reveals the fact the paschimottanasana is much better than this.

Benefits

- It cuts down the intensity of pains in the backbone.
- It makes the backbone more pliant or flexible.
- It is a good preparation for the chakrasana or wheel pose.
- It plays an important role in correcting the displaced navel or other parts of the stomach in proper position.

Home Remedies

- Give up fatty food, and take to abstemiousness with a hard physical labour.
- Physical labour can be substituted by sun salutation (Dog forward backward) pose, etc.
- Honey and lemon juice mixed in tepid water works for slimming the body. Tepid water if taken in the morning and evening can also help to reduce corpulence.
- Fasting with either boiled water or lemon juice, orange juice, any fruit or vegetable juice accompanied with a physical activity is the surest way of getting rid of a pot belly.

34. Easy and Painless Delivery

It is interesting to experience the fact that there are some poses which are very easy but have a very serious impact on the human body. Upturned tree pose is an example. This pose is done by the Yoginis (female Yoga practitioners) especially. The pregnant women can perform this pose even up to eight months of her pregnancy, the structure of the pose does not put the child in the womb in any trouble. This pose is also called tarasana by some sages. Tara means 'stars'.

Tarasana

Because in the tree pose, the entire economy is upturned therefore, some call it an upturned tree pose. As the two palms raised in the sky look like stars, it is called tarasana.

When this pose is practised by pregnant women, the ovary is kept free from unwanted wind. Thus, the child is not affected but rather finds it easy to live in the congested filthy part of the body. The suffocation of the nascent body in the womb which has the characteristic of living in the uterine is eased or is less painful with the help of this pose. As for the mental effect on the child, because the mother's mind is supposed to be connected with spirituality or Yoga, the child also feels blessed. The child in the

Easy and Painless Delivery

womb suffocates in proportion to the negative thoughts that haunt the mother's mind.

In India and in some other countries, a pregnant woman is kept with sanctity, physical comfort and mental balance so that she can produce healthy children. The mother is supposed to maintain a strict careful diet and lifestyle during pregnancy.

Tarasana

Procedure

- Just stand erect – absolutely erect with your chest puffed up with the inhalation of a quantity of air (oxygen).
- Now, you stand on your toes.
- Initially you can take the help of a pillar.
- Slowly start doing it without any support.
- Raise your hands exactly parallel to your head. Maintain the stay. You may bend a little towards any side right or left while keeping your hands in the same parallel position as much as possible. Another way is that standing erect, one hand can be put at the thigh and the other hand raised to the sky and the body slightly curved but not bent (for bending will have injurious effect on the child). Make sure that the body does not bend forward or backward from the waist to the throat but a little sideways only.

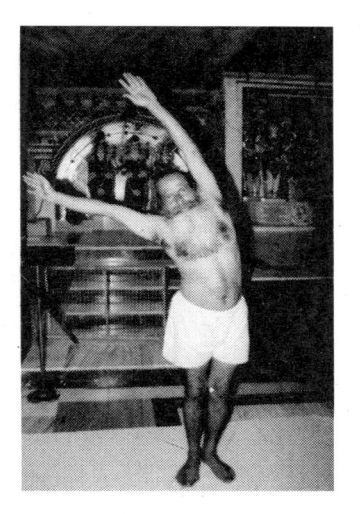

Tarasana

There is one more variation to this asana. While standing on one leg, the other leg can be lifted high and taken backwards. Some call this pose by another name – peepalasana (peepal is a sacred tree of India). The variations are done to remove the monotony but the main principle of the pose (any yoga pose) should not be violated to damage the very purpose of an asana. Pregnant women when they bend forward or backward give a lot of unbearable trouble to the child who is already facing affliction or suffocation. The pose can also be done by standing on the toes and lifting the two hands up and maintaining the stay for some time. The result is the same.

Benefits

The following are the most encouraging blessings of this pose.

(i) According to the intuitive knowledge of the ancient sages and the scriptures it corrects the constitution of the ovary. The ovary being the breeding ground of creatures becomes so free from all kinds of physiological negativities.

(ii) The most striking feature of this pose in the case of women is that they face no trouble both in bearing, i.e. conceiving children, nor do they feel any physical hardship during delivery. As the name of the posture suggests, so is the beauty, and merits of this asana.

Legend goes that Droupadi (a character in the Mahabharata) was a practitioner of this pose.

Home Remedies

- Sesame oil and mustard oil mixed nicely with each other should be used for massaging the tummy and back of a pregnant woman for an easy delivery. It is subjected to experimental verification.
- Powdered asafoetida mixed in six or seven tablespoons of clarified butter, if taken by a pregnant women paves the way for an easy delivery.
- Maintain a stressfree life.

Easy and Painless Delivery

- Waist should not be tightened by belts, ropes and similar things. Tightening of the belts produces the possibility of giving birth to infirm, defective or diseased babies.
- To go without food for a long time is not good. Keep eating at small intervals.
- Oily foods should be taken sparingly.
- Sexual activities should be avoided during pregnancy.
- Lemon juice is reported to be highly beneficial for pregnant women who have retching almost every day. The disease is called morning sickness by the western world. Water with lemon juice and a pinch of rocksalt mixed into it should be taken several times in a day especially morning and evening.
- Pineapple is not good for pregnant women. Many Indian doctors prohibit it.
- At night, the pregnant women should bandage the soles of their feet with a thick cotton so that ovarian problems are held in check or, they could keep their legs on a cotton made pillow all the night or, the soles of the feet should be nicely smeared with tepid mustard oil to avoid cold, etc. To keep the soles warm is itself a guard against ill health.
- If there is problem in lactation then sugar candy (jaggery) and crushed cumin seeds should be mixed in milk and consumed two to three times a day. The first and the last dose should be on an empty stomach and bed time respectively. During the treatment the patient should use a little more turmeric in the vegetables. A lot of water should be taken. This treatment should be followed for about two to four days only.

35. Dyspepsia or Indigestion

The various poses or asanas helpful in dyspepsia are rolling, veepareet karani mudra, shoulder stand, plough pose, locust pose, wheel pose, paschimottanasana, agnisar dhouti, yoga mudra, (special attention) maha mudra, head stand. Peacock pose is another greatest remedy against indigestion for it improves the functioning of the pancreas to the required level. For some reasons the pancreas falls short of a requisite amount of heat which is produced by this posture. The pose looks like a peacock when the legs are raised to the sky as much as possible.

Mayurasana (Peacock Pose)

Procedure

(Be prepared to fall down many times; therefore do not keep anything in the pocket of the garment worn).

- Kneel down.
- Lean forward and press your navel with your elbows.

Mayurasana (Peacock Pose)

Dyspepsia or Indigestion

- Touch the head to the ground.
- Join the elbows so that the fingers of your hands are placed towards your thighs.
- Try to lift up one of your legs while the pressure on your navel by the elbows continues.
- After some days, try to do this with both legs simultaneously. It will take a few or some days to command over this pose. Stick to the practice patiently.

Benefits

- This pose increases the strength of the arms like the tree pose, sun salutation and others.
- It is also beneficial for eyes also.
- Heart and lungs are nicely pressed indirectly and are, therefore toned up internally.
- Problems related to stomach can also be overcome by this pose.

Temporary Domestic Remedies

- Allopathic liver tonics are allowed for some days.
- Ginger juice and a pinch of rock salt half an hour before a meal is good for digestion.
- Both agnisar dhuati and veepareet karani mudra are powerful poses for the purpose. To make the veepareet karani mudra a complete round, the next three poses – shoulder stand, plough pose and fish pose – are needed to be done one after another or otherwise the cycle would remain incomplete and hence the result would not be optimum.
- Use radish (raw) with salt (preferably rock salt in the dining table).

Speaking of Curing Diseases through Yoga

- Lemon juice, rock salt and black pepper – a mixture of these three (also mix ginger) strengthens the digestive capacity.
- Lemon juice a little before the meals is good for digestion. One glass of water with one lemon squeezed in it could also be recommended.
- A mixture of carrot juice, salt, coriander, cumin seeds, black salt, lemon juice and ginger powder is of great help to digest food.
- Carrot is highly beneficial for eyes also. It strengthens the power of eyes too.

36. Loss of Strength in the Arms

Uneven circulation of blood is one of the greatest cause of this problem. When the circulation of blood is impeded on account of various factors, the affected part raises some symptoms out of which weakness is one. However, the following methods will solve the problem:

- Tone up the whole body from crown to the fingers of the legs.
- Beat all parts (beat gently) in the same way.
- Beat a little violently (from neck to the toes).
- Tie two iron rings on a strong branch of a tree. Swing with it as a cradle from one end to the other for more than thirty minutes every day. This will not only improve the strength of your arms but if you are below thirty five years of age your height would also be increased by this. The practice should be done on an empty stomach 4 to 5 hours after having meal.

Other Recommended Postures

- Dog forward and backward and squatting.
- Tree pose which means standing on the hands. The pose looks like a tree as if the branches are legs, the body is the trunk. Since trees have branches, the legs if stretched out carelessly would resemble a tree. In addition to strengthening the arms, it has the following beneficial returns.

Benefits of Tree Pose

- It opens up the blocked nasal passage as soon as it is performed.
- It also evacuates accumulated wind of the stomach, if any.
- On account of the upturned position of the body, the heart, the lungs or respiratory passages responsible for pumping blood to the entire body become properly functional and therefore, serve as a great advantage to the entire economy; therefore highly useful to patients of heart and lungs. But they should be cautious of doing vigorously all of a sudden.
- Eyes are highly affected in a positive way. It is a guard against complaints of the eyes.

37. Semen Preservation

Toe Kissing While Standing

Procedure
- Stand erect.
- Set your feet on the ground by maintaining some distance.
- Now bend forward and try to touch your head to the ground. Turn left or right as you like, and try to kiss the big toes of the legs.
- Do the same with the other leg too.

Toe Kissing While Standing

Speaking of Curing Diseases through Yoga

Home Remedies

- The seed of basil should be eaten with a glass of cold water before going to bed.
- The patient should eat less at night and meditate before sleeping at night.
- Pungent foods or drinks including spices, garlic, fried onion, red dry chilly, tobacco, alcoholic beverages and coffee or tea can welcome the disease.
- Ayurvedic and homeopathic medicines work effectively.

Other Useful Postures

- Padangustha pose
- Expansion of legs
- Tree pose
- Yoga mudra
- Brahmacharya pose (Celibacy pose)
- Headstand pose
- Siddhasana (Success pose).
- Meditation or Japa (counting the heads of a rosary by memorising the mantra – the holy sound given by your teacher, if any) while sitting in the success pose is of a greatest value.

38. Skin Diseases

Impure blood is the root cause of skin diseases. Blood becomes impure mainly on account of intake of wrong food, and an unhealthy lifestyle. In fact, Yoga practitioners do not suffer from this disease for a long period of time, even if they are unfortunately attacked with this complaint for some unavoidable reasons.

Fasting with pure cow (properly boiled) milk, vegetables, fruits or water is the first remedy. Along with this, all kinds of medicines, if possible should be used – Allopathic, Ayurvedic, Herbal or Homeopathic etc. so that the intensity of the disease could be brought to a grinding halt. The following are the recommended Yoga techniques:

Recommended Yoga Postures
- Sun Salutation (till sweating)
- Squatting (till an unbearable pain is felt)
- Narishodhanasana is also very helpful
- Paschimottan pose (minimum 5 minutes without break)
- Wheel pose
- Peacock (5 minutes)
- Tree pose
- Head stand
- Yoga mudra
- Cow mouth

Speaking of Curing Diseases through Yoga

- Scorpion pose is another greatest physiological sword for this pose. The most remarkable feature of this posture is to purify the quality of blood as well as the circulatory system.

Although all the said postures are guaranteed process for the purpose, this pose has a special room for this complaint as experience shows.

It is as tree pose except that the two legs should be brought towards the top of the head in course of time. Doers having a short structure, i.e. whose backbone is not long enough to curve as desired should not be worried, because it works definitely and internally when an attempt to bring the leg to the head is made. The doers having a long backbone do it at ease without any difficulty. One should stay in this pose for a period of time according to the capacity.

Hastapadasana

The pose, however, has some more hygienic advantages:

- It strengthens the arm naturally.
- It guards throat and eye diseases because the parts connected with these organs are so internally massaged that the negative elements find it difficult to make their dwelling houses in the economy.

Some simplest Yoga techniques (Kriyas) will definitely help to protect, or eradicate skin diseases. These processes can be followed even without the help of a Yoga teacher.

After the expiry of about five hours of a square meal, the patient should go to a lonely place, toilet, bathroom, bush, etc. penetrate slowly the middle finger of his right hand. If there is

Skin Diseases

any undigested food stuff or negative elements contained in the stomach, it will come out of mouth, or if there is no such thing, only water would be coming out without any offensive odour:

This process guards the patient from being attacked with any stomach diseases in future. This process can also be done at any time, if the patient feels complaints in his stomach.

(Another way) Live either on boiled water or on fruit juices for 24 hours. No solid food should be taken for at least 24 hours.

Early in the morning, boil about litres of water. When boiled keep it aside, mix lemon juice (2 lemons are enough). Strain the water with a piece of a clean cloth and mix a reasonable amount of common salt or rock salt in the water in your mouth till the water reaches almost your throat. Go to a bathroom and insert the middle finger of your right hand (next to the thumb).

Caution – the nails of the finger must be paired nicely so as to avoid minor injury of laceration of the throat or mouth. Be cautious.

You will start retching and, then giving away i.e. vomiting the salted water you had taken time and again; go on inserting your said finger. You may also feel the urge to relieve yourself.

Lie down in a dead pose for a while. Break your fasting with either (a) fruit juice (b) curd or khichari (A combination of rice, lentils, sufficient quantity of vegetables, spinach plus butter or cheese; you may eat one dishful with your heart's content).

Your stomach would be free from being attacked from any complaints – pain, worms, inflammation, acidity all your life.

Appendicitis, ulcers etc. can be held in check, protected or even cured if the dietetic rules are strictly followed. The process is open to all ages if the patient can follow the way. It should be done once in 20 days or even fortnight. Dry chilly is worse than worst. Green chilly may be used instead; but the best is black pepper.

Arctium Lapa, a homeopathic medicine, which is generally used for purifying the blood. The clear name is Arctium Lapa 200 (if the skin disease is more than a year then two drops or even three drops).

Home Remedies

- Drop about 60 gms of neem leaves into the overheated mustard oil. The leaves would start turning black. Now allow the oil to cool down. Strain it and smear the oil on the eczema affected spots 4 or 5 times a day. It works.
- A quantity of camphor mixed with coconut oil should be rubbed on the affected area.
- Seven or eight Neem (margosa) leaves swallowed on an empty stomach early in the morning also works for purification of blood. Fifteen to twenty neem leaves fried in mustard oil could be eaten with rice before a meal for several days.
- Black pepper and a reasonable quantity of clarified butter (butter when boiled for some minutes becomes clarified) should be mixed with a little crushed black pepper and smeared on the affected parts of eczema or itching, etc.
- The seed of a radish should be crushed and made a pest by mixing a little water so that it could be heated.
- Fresh basil leaves, if mixed with lemon juice smeared on the eczema spots is beneficial.
- Lemon juice mixed with mint is good. It should be drunk and not smeared.

39. Heavy Posterior

Padangustha Nasaparshasana

Procedure

- Lie on your back and stretch out both the legs to the fullest.
- Pull your left foot with your left hand and bring it close to the nose.
- Do it with the other leg following the same way.
- You have to do this every day to make it a success.

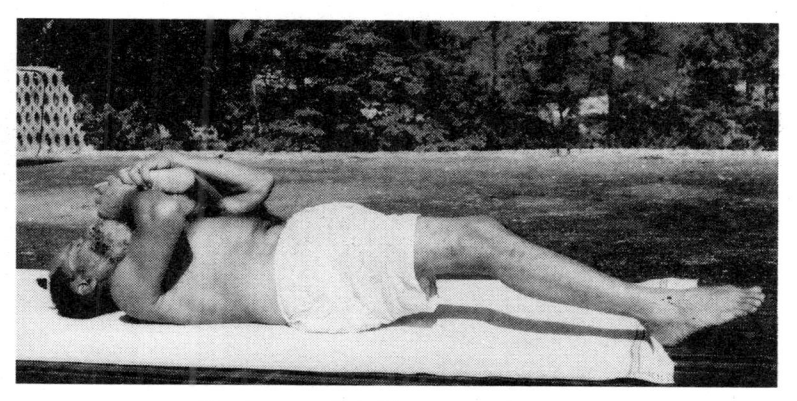

Padangustha Nasaparshasana

However, other recommended postures are:

- Paschimottanasana pose
- Sun salutation and squatting (special attention to squatting; thrice the sun salutation in this case)

Speaking of Curing Diseases through Yoga

- Locust pose
- Bow pose, expansion of legs etc.
- Skipping, jogging in a mountainous place are other best useful and guaranteed remedies

Dietetic Remedies

- Avoid stuffy food absolutely.
- Live only on fruit and vegetables juices.
- Night food except for a liquid food is not congenial.
- Honey is useful for this complaint. Honey with a glass of hot water should be consumed every day. Abstemiousness is a great virtue in this case.
- Lemon juice with water every day is said to have a slimming effect.

All these recommendations should be followed, however, (i) sun salutation (ii) squatting (iii) bow pose are most preferable recommendations.

Like Uttanpadasana, camel pose, etc. this pose also is a great remedy against a displaced navel. The patient should perform this posture many times with repeated rests in the mean time.

Dietetic inhibitions are more important than asanas in this case. To take resort to measures that slim the body in a few weeks or days is to invite adverse repercussions sooner or later for, a fastest change in the economy is not natural but artificial. Hatha Yoga in this case, however, works more nicely than any other system, however regular yoga practitioners are never a victim of this ludicrous complaint. It is sad to see the plight of some ignorant women who walk in an ugly gait with their posterior as high as mountains. Posterior has been made by the Almighty to meditate on Him for hours or to work some virtuous deeds but, it is highly regrettable, some people have it as a burden as if it is borne by a porter.

40. Increase Your height

Trikonasana (Triangular Pose)

If proper attempts are made in early childhood or at an adult age; height can be increased to a minimum of 5 to 6 inches. Medicinal remedies are hardly of any help. The best way in this case is physical and physiological measures.

Triangular pose has been found to be working for many victims.

Procedure

- Stand astride by maintaining a distance of about two and a half feet.
- Raise both your hands to the sky.
- Now bend on one side touching the leg with one hand while the other hand is extended up in the sky.
- Stay in this position for sometime.

Trikonasana (Triangular Pose)

Caution

The waist should not be moved or turned. Practise swinging to reach the destined spot (to catch the foot).

In addition to this pose, swinging with two iron rings hung and tied with the branch of a tree or an iron bar is also very helpful.

Speaking of Curing Diseases through Yoga

The swinging should be done twice a day. Somebody's help is needed to push the body to be swung from one end to the other. It should be done twice a day for a period of time. Other complaints, namely, deformities of body structure and constipation, etc. can also be tackled and cured through this asana.

41. Spleen Disease

Spleen is an abdominal organ maintaining proper conditioning of the blood. The conditioning of blood implies natural or the right proportion of red blood corpuscles and white blood corpuscles, and other constituents that form the blood. Spleen when affected becomes harder, bigger, swollen, sensitive, etc. It is also connected with malaria fever. When it is enlarged it is called spleenitis. It causes loose motions and leads to inflammation of the stomach. The whole body, hands, feet, etc. become lean and thin and emaciated.

Home Remedies

- Radish (also radish leaves, especially green leaves) mixed with black salt (a pinch or a few pinches) is a useful herbal remedy against spleen complaints (black salt and rock salt are not same). The remedy should be taken on an empty stomach.
- One cup of radish juice with three or four pinches of black salt thrice a day for several days also helps.
- Radish is a great remedy for jaundice. Radish leaves should be mixed with sugar candy (purified sugar), about half a tea cup (or a little more than this) and four or five teaspoons of sugar candy for about a month or so. Milk and turmeric are prohibited for any possible recurrence.
- Ripe papaya is a useful remedy against jaundice. Papaya is useful for liver and stomach. The juice of green papaya is also equally remedial.

- The fever of any sort could be treated at home. Lemon tea (black tea) is a useful remedy. Lemon juice with rock salt is a great remedy for malaria.
- To guard against a spleen disease, the patient should stop the rise of body temperature in the first instance. In addition to the success pose there are some home remedies against fever, e.g. a combination of basil leaves, black pepper and lemon juice is a useful remedy against temperature.

The pose that guards spleen disease is called nari shodhanasana. Its function is to purify the naris. Naris, in Sanskrit, are the invisible canals spread throughout the body for the purpose of carrying the vital force (prana) in an even way. If this pose is done, the body remains free from the disturbance caused by uneven supply of blood in the body and other functional disorders.

Other Remedies
- A herbal medicine named Arctium Lappa 200, available in the U.S.A. and most probably elsewhere in the world, has been in use by many Americans as a blood purifying agent. Two or three drops of Arctium Lappa 200 can be taken if the skin disease is as old as one year.
- In addition to ayurvedic remedies, green turmeric (half the size of a finger) plus treacle are eaten every day on an empty stomach to bolster or purify the blood in a most natural way. A decoction of mint, ginger or basil also works for malaria which is connected with spleen disorders.

A decoction of bitter gourd, half a tea cup, is also blood purifying in case of skin infections, urinary complaints, etc.

Narishodhanasana

Procedure
- Stand up and lift your hands and straighten them..

Spleen Disease

- Start leaning forward and try to touch the ground. Initially start reaching out for the shins.
- Stay in this posture for some time, make sure you do not bend your legs.
- Slowly start raising your hands above the head.
- Now slowly bend backward taking both the hands behind. You will gradually improve bending backwards.
- When your hands are brought above your head, lean right or left as you like; but lean on both sides keeping one hand close to the head.
- By performing the pose at the front, back, right and left side, one full round of the pose is done. Do it several times or stay in each position for a long time with the retention of your breath – a fact which is normal and effective for producing the optimum result. Bear in mind retention is the source of blessings for any yoga posture.

Children can do it very nicely and easily. Without any hesitation, they bend their bodies like a cane could be made half-round or even more and still it does not break. People whose backbones are not very long or, in other words, who are not tall, find it difficult to reach the backside to the greatest optimum extent but however, the construction of backbone being same for any human being tall or short, the result arising out of the bending of the backbone is same. So, there is no cause for worry.

Benefits

The following are the benedictions of this asana.
- It is a strong guard against spleen diseases – spleenitis, etc.
- The blood is purified so there are no skin diseases. It is a strong guard against skin diseases although there are some more asanas for it.
- It protects senility which is caused by congestion of the backbone with negative and filthy substances.

Speaking of Curing Diseases through Yoga

- It helps the vital wind to flow undisturbed on account of unobstructed naris (subtle arteries and veins).
- In addition to physiological or hygienic benefits, the pose brings forth innerness or introversion in a shortest period of time on the ground that the vital wind (prana) which has two directions – one being downward and the other upward – comes to a uniform state – a fact which indicates that the prana has run into the sushumna , for the prana without having any access to the sushumna cannot bring forth introversion – the most covetous aim of a Yogi.

Other Recommended Yoga Postures

- Paschimottanasana
- Chakrasana
- Tarasana
- Scorpion pose
- Suryanamaskar
- Singhasana

42. Maha Mudra

Mudra is a metaphor for the word 'coin' which is a must for marketing. It is called mahamudra on the ground of the fact that it hits the base of the backbone at which the mooldhara is situated.

Maha Mudra

Procedure

- Sit erect.
- Stretch out your legs fully.
- Fold one of the legs in such a way that the heel touches the dehamadhya.
- Make sure you sit carefully on your heel.
- Set the sole of the feet parallel to the other thigh.
- Now, with your hands try to catch the foot of the leg lying stretched out. The elbow should be on the ground and the nose must touch the knee. Don't forget to do the mool bandh (closure of anus). Neither exhale nor inhale in the staying position. This is one part of the pose. Rest of the part should be done by the other leg.

Benefits

- Mahamudra is done at the end of the asanas when the physiology or kundalini part (situated at the anus) is warm enough to produce the requisite impetus. When the perineum (dehamadhya) is pressed forcefully, the doer feels a spirit of introversion as per the laws of nature.

- Restfulness is the penultimate object of Yoga while the ultimate mission is consciousness. Without the former, the latter cannot be achieved so this mudra is called maha mudra.
- Its benefits are a little more and direct as compared to Paschimottanasana. Unlike the Paschimottanasana, it is done at the end of many postures. Introversion is the mission of this pose.
- It relieves backache.
- It makes the back more supple.

If the doer gasps while doing this pose, then it means the doer lacks yogic health but this pose corrects breathing in the first place. While doing this pose make sure that the inhalation is equal to exhalation. Gradually inhalation would increase. In transcendence, however the doer is beyond the boundary of respiration because it is within the boundary of senses only.

43. Asana for General Health and Well-being

There was a great Yogi in India. He vanished his divine body only some years ago. His name was Deo Raha Baba. Baba means a saint or yogi but the words Deo Raha convey a special significance. It signifies the fact that he lived his life absolutely beware of his flesh and blood and was always in a state of divine intoxication. There is a big railway station after his name. He was said to have a successful command over the kechari moodra (the moodra that helps one to leave this sensory world for the sky and live mentally up above the azure).

His holiness used to advise this pose for the maintenance of health and the scriptures advocate his instruction fully. Yoga mudra is the pose He used to advise.

Yog Mudra

Procedure
- Sit in the lotus pose.
- Now, catch all the toes of your legs by crossing your hands, i.e. right toes with the right hand, and the left toes with the left hand.
- Exhale and empty your stomach.

Yog Mudra

Speaking of Curing Diseases through Yoga

- Slowly bend and try to touch the ground with your nose and maintain the stay; the more the time of stay, the better.

Benefits

- It improves the digestive capacity. It is no less than the peacock pose or sun salutation. Dyspeptic patients can depend on it.
- Patients suffering from hernia, orchitis, etc. are advised to do this, because the arteries and veins, connected with the genital organs etc. are strained, massaged and toned up.

Other Measures

- To maintain health, triphala churan should be taken twice daily. It is an Ayurvedic remedy which can be taken all life by any one for the maintenance of health.
- Get up early in the morning.
- Meditate on the bed even before responding to the call of Nature unless it is too urgent.
- Practise Yoga exercises for a time depending on an individual's capacity.
- Practise Yoga in the evening or night too or meditate only.

Diet

- Eat more vegetables and less of starchy food. Try to avoid meat and alcohol as much as possible. Fresh fish, sea fish are good for health. It contains a lot of iodine, etc. It improves eyesight too. Avoid eating dry chilly and stale food.
- Meat is an acid food. It requires more time to get digested. It improves flesh but produces diseases in course of time. Egg produces excessive wind and sexual excitement especially at a young age. It is better to avoid egg as much as one can.
- Try to restrain from sexual activities as far as possible.

44. Loss of Appetite

Both hunger and thirst are the outbursts of health. The more the pancreas is active, sooner the victims feel hungry and thirsty. Out of the Yoga postures that activate the pancreas most, Veepareet Karani Mudra is top ranking. When this pose is done, the entire pancreas turns upside down, i.e. the system of the pancreas is changed vigorously. It creates or manufactures a kind of heat which is responsible for creating hunger or thirst of the patient. It is also called preparatory shoulder stand for the latter can be done in one attempt without a break. In shoulder stand, the parts of the body right from shoulders to the feet stand perpendicular on the ground while the hands may or may not support the waist against falling, while in the case of the Veepareet Karani Mudra, looks like a plough from the shoulder to the waist.

As for the function, the Veepareet Karani has its impact on the pancreas mainly, and the shoulder stand effects all parts of the body vigorously well up to the throat, to say the least. The shoulder stand is called sarvangasana which means, 'asana of all parts of the body'. With eyes closed, and the MB (Moolbandh) followed respectfully, one can enter the supra sensory domain if he is sincerely sincere. Both the sarvangasana and the veepareet karani mudra are restricted to the patients suffering from high blood pressure. They should watch their feelings while they practise the asana in consultation with a physician. The sarvangasana has however, the following beautiful fruits:

Benefits of Sarvangasana
- It helps to correct the displacement of navel.
- The veepareet karani also has the same effect.

Speaking of Curing Diseases through Yoga

- Ovarian complaints, namely, uneasiness, pain, retching or vomiting, etc. are either strongly guarded or even completely relieved in a short span of time. Ovarian complaints being relieved, the health of the victim is restored naturally. As for male devotees, stomach, the store house of diseases, is stirred heavily capacitating to evacuate unwanted negative wind by stirring the filthy substances. Both men and women having bulky waist will surely be benefited. The backbone is kept in a healthy condition without any difficulties.
- Plasticity of the backbone a fact which is a must for health is maintained.
- Bulky posterior is also transformed into a beautiful shape.
- Skin eruptions, skin diseases or skin problems are greatly protected and cured.
- Flaccidity of the body is controlled.

Because this pose has a direct bearing upon the shoulder in which a heavy amount of blood is accumulated; it is necessary to follow it up with plough pose and fish pose. Therefore, most sages are of the opinion that veepareet karani, shoulder stand, plough pose and fish pose should be done one after another. They also point out that the time to be spent in the fish pose should be nearly half the time taken by the combined poses from veepareet to plough pose or otherwise the victim may suffer from shoulder diseases namely, spondilitis, neck ache, backache, etc.

As for appetite, both the postures veepareet karani and shoulder stand have an equal contribution.

Veepareet Karani Mudra

Procedure
- Lie on the back.
- Stretch out the two legs fully.

Loss of Appetite

- Lift up the parts of your body – from waist to the feet with your hands. while the parts – from shoulder to the waist form an angle of about 45° or legs should be absolutely straight, while the waist would be supported by the hands strongly. This is what is called Veepareet Karani which literally means 'to upturn' (the lower part of the body). One should stay for a considerable period of time to derive the maximum return.

Veepareet Karani Mudra

Sarvangasana or Shoulder Stand

- Now, the 45° angle (from the shoulder to the waist) is needed to be raised absolutely straight so that head to the end of the neck is parallel to the ground and the entire body from the toes to the throat is absolutely perpendicular to the shoulder. So, this pose is called shoulder stand. Some people can do this asana without the support of the hands; some do it with the support of hands. Old people find it a little difficult to lift up the body without the support, if the practice is not regular. But the results are same. From the toe to the shoulder, the body should be exactly 90 degrees perpendicular to the ground although such a perfect state is done mostly by young men and women only.

Shoulder Stand or Sarvangasana

Speaking of Curing Diseases through Yoga

Benefits

Advantages of the pose are as same as or in a little higher degree in respect of the appetite pose; the only difference is that the shoulder stand covers all the parts of the body in a greater way than the veepareet karani which is called mudra and not asana perfectly.

Other Remedies

- The best way is to climb up a mountain to work in an agricultural field – spading, digging or breaking some stones till you start sweating.
- Drink one glass of water mixed with lemon juice to rouse the appetite. Ginger may also be mixed with it.

Ayurvedic Remedies

- Triphalachuran, an Ayurvedic remedy which has been mentioned in the book many times – is also useful to use immediately after a meal. Triflachuran is advisable to fight any complaint or to maintain health. It should be taken two times (2 teaspoonfuls each time) morning and evening.
- Sun salutation works nicely to fight loss of appetite.
- Loss of appetite is an indication of internal disorderliness especially stomach. Therefore, stomach problem-related asanas, exercises should be emphasised.
- Stomach cleaning processes as detailed in the skin disease pose should be followed.
- A mixture of ginger, lemon juice and rock salt is said to rouse the appetite.
- Carrot juice mixed with rock salt, black pepper, ginger, coriander, cumin and lemon juice (especially) also rouses appetite.

Veepareet Karani Mudra, shoulder stand and the head stand poses are in a way useful at least from one point of view. In all

Loss of Appetite

these postures, the body is more or less turned upside down (the words Veepareet Karani itself suggest the meaning). By turning the body upside down, the nectar oozes at the palate of the mouth – a fact for which foods taste delicious but the nectar energy so gained from the navel is devoured up by the navel at which the power of the sun god pervades – a fact as to why man becomes old after an age. If these poses as said earlier are done, the position of the powers of the sun god and the nectar turns just the reverse; that is to say, the Nectar is no more destroyed by the sungod power, hence the practitioner can save the nectar energy every day and cut down the aging process of the Nature to an extent by accumulating the power every day.

As a matter of caution, it can be advised that even these poses are helpful in accumulating energy, it should not be done for a long period of time for the sole purpose of acquiring energy from this particular pose only, because the Yogins of the yore are of the opinion that for such positions of body in which the body is turned upside down especially the head stand pose, a strict continence or celibacy should be maintained or else, the benedictions of Yoga may be transformed into afflictions or diseases especially mental. Besides, sufficient butter, milk, etc. should be taken by the practitioner, especially beginners.

This is a warning for the good of the self-styled Yogins having no teacher or guru on account of self-conceit possessed by their ignorance which may have to be compensated by incurable diseases. So, beware of self-conceit.

45. Pain in the Neck

The shoulder stand being done, the next pose should be plough pose on the ground so that the blood accumulated in the neck is evenly distributed, and the cranium or otherwise, the doer may face spondilitis (or some call spondilosis). There may be some other reasons as to why the ancient scriptures and the personal experiences also advocate this advice (to follow the plough pose immediately after the shoulder stand). In addition to this, the chest at which lungs and heart – the two most important parts of a human body – are situated, is nicely massaged internally. This process has a heavy impact on the lungs and the heart, to be precise.

Hare pose, head stand, karnapeerasana, bow pose, and Chakrasana are other useful asanas.

Home Remedies

- Rice poultice may be used to foment the pain in neck. Cook some rice and keep it in a piece of cloth or in a small bag or pouch. Foment the affected parts with it and also put cold water alternatively. It should work in most cases.
- Some herbal oils are also useful.
- Keep a pillow in the sun for few hours, and then foment the part with it. Keep repeating the process.
- Burn some wooden fuel strain it and let the wooden charcoal be thrown away, only the heated ashes should be used. Keep it in a rag and then bandage the affected part at night. The ashes should not have unbearable heat. Lie down and sleep. It may be called heat therapy – absolutely domestic but it works nicely.

Pain in the Neck

- For other parts of the body if affected by sprain, the some remedy can be used.

Diet

- No fast food or fatty food after the sunset.
- Fruit juices or vegetables juice should be taken.
- Milk should be consumed with few pieces of garlic in it.

Some Exercises

- Move your neck forward and back ward and right and left several times.
- Also rotate the neck clockwise and anticlockwise.
- Perform all these every day time or whenever you sit for meditation.

Neck problem is sometimes caused by a defective way of placing the neck at the pillow. One should lie down on the bed in the left hand side in which the alimentary canal (the food carrying zone) is situated. One hand should be at the pillow not touching the chest and the other, on the right leg thigh. The hands touching the chest disturb the function of the heart and the victim may face nightmare.

To avoid nightmare, one fragrant incense stick should be kept burning to chase away apparitions or ghosts. But the prayer should be fervent to avoid nightmares. The best way is to meditate or to perform Japa (counting the rosary).

Hare Pose

Procedure

- Kneel down.
- Keep bending forward.
- Now, catch the heels with your hands. Don't sit but bend like the back of a hare (an elevated or lifted up back to a

point forming almost a cone). Bend more and more but strictly maintaining the hold of the heels; don't release them. Stay in this position for sometime.

Other Remedies

- Locust pose, wheel pose, nari shodhasana, mahamudra headstand, rest pose
- Fasting (having boiled water only)
- Fomentation with rice poultice
- Ayurvedic or allopathic massaging oils or ointments
- One glass of hot water with one teaspoon of fenugreek seeds (early in the morning or bed time especially) is also helpful
- Heat therapy
- Make the habit of sitting erect always
- Sleep on cotton-filled mattresses only

In addition to all these processes, the victim should follow, if possible all the systems of medicines. Allopathic system of medicine may be used to beat down the intensity in the first instance. One teaspoon of garlic juice plus one lemon squeezed in half a cup of water and half a teaspoon of dry ginger powder mixed, if taken twice or thrice a day for few days immediately after food, works satisfactorily.

46. Fidgeting

Weak heart, ill health, under nourished economy, lack of nutritious food, etc. are the main causes of fidgeting. If these main causes are treated, fidgeting would also be cured automatically. There are some poses which help a particular part of the body to get rid of fidgeting. Tolangula asana is a remedy against the fidgety fingers while hastapadasana or is a remedy against fidgety legs.

Cycling and Anti-cycling for Fidgety Legs

- Lie on your back.
- Lift your head about six inches from the ground.
- Lift your legs too and move them as if you are riding a bicycle. Move them clockwise and then anticlockwise. Move them as fast as you can.
- Tapot and beat up your thighs/legs as if you are an expert masseur. Beat for more than twenty minutes. Beat the joints more. You are, however, at liberty to take the help of someone.

Other Useful Poses

- Stand up on the toes only; better avoid all kinds of support; stand and stay for time.
- Perform Suryanamaskar till you sweat or gasp profusely if needful, have rest and do it again. This is a way to build stamina.
- Squatting four times with repeated rests.

Speaking of Curing Diseases through Yoga

- Expansion of legs. Stay in this pose as long as it is comfortable. The pose would work as a medicinal dose. Greater the pains, nearer the cure.

Initially practise these for a short period of time and then gradually increase the time period.

Other Remedies

- Massaging with herbal oil will only help temporarily.
- Slowly increase the intake of nutritious foods and drinks.
- Germinated grams, wheat saplings are highly useful to improve the condition.
- Hastapadasana (hands touch feet) is a good pose. It is a part of Narishodhanasana.

Hastapadasana

Procedure

- Stand up and raise your hands.
- Slowly take them back and then bring them to the former position.
- Now bend down slowly to touch the feet.

Caution

The body structure must not be curved but from the waist to the head. Bend and try to touch your feet. This being finished, slowly release your hands and come back to former position (with hands lifted up at the ears) and bend backwards to compensate the forwarding posture of hands. Repeat it as many times as you can.

Hands should also touch below knees. Practise it by swinging up and down every day. So, to clarify, the hands in this pose should move forward touching the knees.

Homoeopathic medicines work nicely for many diseases but since the remedies vary according to different kinds of symptoms,

Fidgeting

it is not possible to mention all the remedies to restrain the bigness of the volume of this book. Make an arrangement of some pots (preferably earthen). Sow some wheat which would grow into saplings after some days. Use the whole sapling crushing it into juice or mincing and mixing it with green vegetables or with other food stuff like milk, pasta, bread, curd, etc. Naturopaths believe that this gives energy to the human body. It is wise to put the saplings in a shadow, namely in bathroom.

47. Nervousness

There are some Yogic asanas which are helpful in restoring fearlessness or overcoming nervousness. These asanas lift up the total personality of the doer.

Khanjanasana

Recommended postures

- Confidence building pose (Veerasana)
- Peacock pose
- Fearless pose (Kalbhairavi pose)
- Nervousness pose (Khanjanasana)
- Leg trouble pose
- Sun salutation with squatting
- Finger strengthening pose
- Wheel pose

The victim should meditate and think of a lion, tiger, fire, and if he is not an atheist, meditate on his deity or God. If atheist, think on the endless firmament.

He should have the courage to think – I am not the man to fall-back upon, come what may or little do I care unless I am wrong.

Nervousness

Procedure

- Kneel down.
- Raise your hands to shoulder bend and keep them in one straight line parallel to the ground.

I am afraid you are sure to lose your balance and fall down. There is, however, an opinion that your feet should move like the tail of a khanjan bird but in fact, you should not move, for to move while doing a pose of Yoga is not instructed by the sage Patanjali who gives the definition of asanas in the following way. "Sthira Sukhang Asanam" – Asana is a physical state in which there is stillness of body as well as comfort or enjoyment. Besides, to move the legs like the bird concerned is to allow dissipation of mind.

Persons suffering from nervousness have their hearts less strong. To strengthen it, they should follow the yoga asanas connected with improvement of heart, circulation of blood.

Home Remedies

- It is reported that a combined intake of ginger, garlic and honey of a reasonable quantity every day helps relieve both a heart disease as well as a nervous mind.
- Gourd (some call it Jukinee, *louki* in Hindi) and mint with a pinch of black pepper also helps.
- Vegetarians and teetotallers suffer less from this complain.

Nervous people should accept defeat or loss, repeated defeats or loss would boost up their morale gradually. They should take initiative and see the result, come what may.

48. Sleeplessness (Insomnia)

The pose is rightly called dead pose by the sages as it perfectly resembles the dead body of a man perfectly, but this pose can also be called a fatigue cum sleeping posture by virtue of its merits. Howsoever one may be tired of work or exhausted by a laborious work, this pose makes up for the tiredness or exhaustion in a shortest period because the burden of the whole body is not borne by the backbone. Pressure on the back causes exhaustion, tiredness or fatigue. Therefore, as the backbone is set to the ground flat, respiration comes down, giving a span of rest to the lungs functioning less actively than before. Physiologically, respiration, the first work of man, when comes to a lesser number of times, lesser thoughts spring from the mind which is connected with respiration intimately. Quite naturally, therefore, the pose has both hygienic as well as psychological background.

Shavasana

Procedure

- Lie down on your back. Keep your heels juxtapose; keep them at ease without using any force not even the slightest.
- Keep the hands adjacent to the thighs but not on

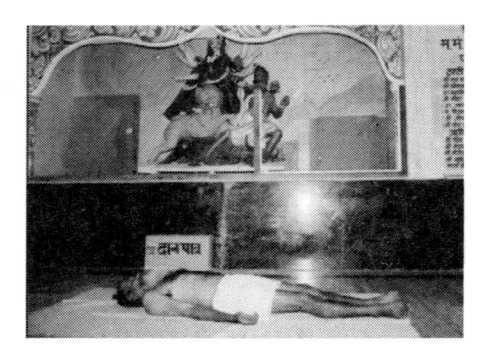

Shavasana (Dead Pose)

Sleeplessness (Insomnia)

the thighs. The palms should be upturned facing the sky. The hands also should be kept easily like the heels are kept. Relax your whole body.
- Close your eyes.
- Think nothing – a fact which is not easily understandable. Therefore, the sages have found out a means – think on the clear sky, firmament or, the macrocosmic vast azure.

The sages have made it possible by dint of tenacious practices only and not by any magic wand. These being done, now, inhale slowly hold your breath for sometime – in the beginning and not for a long time – release it with both the nostrils; do this process repeatedly

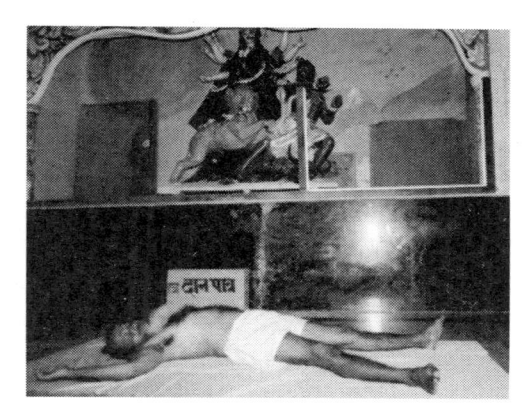

Accidental Dead Pose

with the greater amount of inhalation, retention and exhalation. If you believe in any personal God or deity, you can remember him/ her; if you do not have, the vast firmament is the last resort. The result is exactly the same. If you are a Japa doer, you may use your Japa and make the said process easier and even deeper. Bear in mind, you should not use any pillow which will impede your physiological system. You may fall asleep while doing this asana. In fact, Yoga practitioners sleep less by dint of Yoga blessings. To sleep more than required is not allowed in Yoga. Sleep is tamsik if excessive because man forgets his beloved 'father in the Heaven' during the sleep. His mind which is meant for enjoying His affinity / remembrance, is covered deeply with a great ignorance of unknowingness. It is not darkness but Light which is a premonition of knowledge, the Absolute.

Speaking of Curing Diseases through Yoga

Constipation, stresses and strains, physical complaints, over burdened by mundane thoughts etc. are some of the predisposing causes of sleeplessness. Natural sleeplessness which a good Yogi enjoys is conducive to attain deeper sensorial joy, whereas sleeplessness acquired by artificial medicines narcotics, etc. only makes the economy addicted or attached to drugs which are highly injurious in the long run but are apparently consolatory. While following the said process don't forget the MB.

In the case of removing fatigue too, thinking on the firmament absolutely full of Nothing is the best way, and not just lying down and thinking on some matter, worldly matters, etc. This pose ensures a steady slowing down of all functions of the body including the functioning of the brain and therefore, brings forth peace of mind by and by automatically.

There are pupils who perform this pose with their limbs, hands and heads, etc. in an unmanageable or dissipated way, as if they have been killed in an encounter. No doubt this pose is claimed dead pose; but the fact is that when a dead body is sent to a cremation ground according to any religion, the limbs – hands, feet, head, etc. are set in an organised posture and not in an ugly way. Besides, such a willful neglect of keeping the limbs dissipated requires an amount of physical force and mental willingness which are prohibited in this pose. Thus, any variation other than the most natural as has been prescribed in the ancient scriptures is not admissible, but the ground of breaking the monotonous traditionality however, is allowed for some time.

People suffering from high blood pressure may follow this pose after having a glass of cold water mixed with the juice of one or two lemons.

This pose is connected with the head stand especially. The time of this pose should be about half the time consumed by the head stand, although this pose (dead pose) can be done before or after any pose or exercise, whenever there is a reason to take rest.

Sleeplessness (Insomnia)

The dead pose should be followed both before and after the head stand pose immediately as per the old books and personal experience.

Caution

- Unreasonable delay in breaking the dead pose may lead to torpidity (sluggishness).
- It increases sensuality occasionally.
- This pose also works for evacuation of excessive winds of the stomach and hence it works for pawanmuktasana too.

Mental Benefits

The doer is struck by the thought 'dead' which induces him to enter the kingdom of philosophy – a preliminary step to Yoga. Such a thought helps to destroy the locus standi of mind.

Home Remedies

- A mixture of lemon juice and a pinch of black pepper, honey and water work against sleeplessness.
- Japa or meditation is the best way.
- There are, however, different finger moodras. Some sages are of the opinion that a particular finger technique has a particular remedy against particular physical complaint or disease, namely when the thumb and index finger are joined it is called gyanmudra and is helpful in improving concentration of mind. Like this, there are about ten moodras. To name some – shunya moodra, vayu moodra, chidakash (heart of firmament) moodra, varun moodra, etc.

49. Liver Diseases

Liver is a glandular organ secreting bile. Its colour is dark reddish-brown. The English word 'liverish' stands for peevishness on the ground of the fact that persons suffering from liver troubles which are connected with a fatty degeneration of liver or liver abscess, hepatitis, etc. have a peevish temperament. Bilious is a word derived from the root word bile. Bilious is related to an illness caused by too much bile. Enlargement of liver may be connected with jaundice. Contraction of liver is caused by its failure to exclude the increasing ingredients to mix with the bile. Jaundice, therefore, should not be allowed to became more intense. When the liver is indurated and enlarged (swelled) it becomes really painful. Spicy food or intake of green chillies can cause excessive pain, distension of belly, etc. are the effects of an enlarged liver. The main causes of liver problems are:

- Having too much tea or coffee especially on an empty stomach. It is therefore, advisable to drink two to three glasses of cold water after having fried or fatty food and before the intake of a strong coffee or tea.

- Alcohol is another dangerous poison. On account of addiction, the addicted fails to observe the rules; violation, thus, becomes a habit and the result in the long run is an incurable state in most cases.

- Having too much of spicy food or intake of green chillies can cause ulcer in the stomach or duodenum ulcer.

Doctors opine that liver disease may also be the result, of some then diseases, namely, diabetes, malaria, gout, cancer, enlarged

Liver Diseases

liver, heart diseases (when the disease is dangerously established for a long time).

Home Remedies

- Raw bitter gourd juice on an empty stomach is highly beneficial in jaundice. According to Ayurvedic doctors a person having any liver problem should eat raw turmeric 10 gms or 15 gms every day on an empty. The same rule is applicable for problems related to spleen.

- Liver diseases can be treated positively by a mixture of lemon juice and black pepper as reported by many student observers. It should be taken for about twenty days at least.

- Radish juice (with leaves) with sugar candy and two or three pieces of lemon at bed time every day is also useful. Jaundice is also fought with a mixture of onion juice, lemon juice, rock salt, black pepper. The lemon juice should be several teaspoons in quantity.

- A large quantity of heavily fried fish, vegetables accompanied with an excessive amount of pungent spices costs the normal function of the liver which fails to function properly in course of time. In fact, fried edibles are not good for liver patients at all.

Do's and Don'ts

- The Yoga rule of eating should be absolutely hygienic. Eat half the stomach so that there is enough room for air in the stomach. If the air or wind is too heavy its tendency is to go down and not up, thus, making the respiration (connected with mind) below the navel. The result is obsession with the idea of lower senses than with the upper ones, namely (where the diety lives) heart, head or above the head.

- Diet is more important than or equally important to Yoga asanas which cannot help the patient when the condition is precarious. But after propping up the condition to an extent especially by allopathic or homoeopathic remedies or by both, yoga or concerned postures should be imposed on the body. Ayurveda was discovered at a time when yogic asanas could not be done by patients on account of the intensity of diseases. The liver when becomes too dysfunctional, fails to digest even water which comes out of the mouth immediately. If food is eaten, vomiting is sure and certain in a precarious condition.

The following are the recommended postures for boosting up the capacity of the liver.

- Peacock pose (It should be done for a period of about twenty minutes in one attempt in the beginning days of learning; even if the elbows are put in the navel to press it violently with at least one leg lifting above the ground).
- Sun salutation is another sharp sword to cut off the complaint.
- Matsyendrasana plays an important role in restoring the liver condition.
- Veepareet karani mudra is another asana on account of its strong bearing on the pancreas and liver. The pose should, as per rules follow the next three poses – Shoulder stand and plough pose and the fish pose which should be done for a period which should be half the total time taken by the preceding three postures.
- Every day in addition to stomach cleaning process (once in 20 days), the patient should follow cleaning the stomach through vomiting (see Skin Disease Pose).
- Liver patients are not supposed to work a lot. Rest, meditation, seclusion, abstention from smoking, alcohol, tobacco, etc. are the best ways to protect you further aggravation.

Beneficial are salads, fruits, carrot, lemon juice, rock salt, pomegranate, apple, pineapple (for jaundice) fig, cashew nuts

Liver Diseases

almonds, etc. Juices of green vegetables or fruits with a little ginger and black pepper in it are beneficial.

Meditation or Yogic Kriya

Procedure

- Sit (preferably in the success or in the Lotus Pose). When sitting in an ordinary pose too, the genitalia should be comfortably pressed in such a way that the scrotum feels no injury but comfort. Practise can make it a success.
- Keep the back straight.
- Maintain M.B (closure of anus) or try to pull up the air towards above and then release it, do it repeatedly. This is what is called M.B (mool bundh). It is a kind of mudra- a very secret and sacred key to Yogins.
- Press lightly the navel part towards the back. Needless to say, the stomach should be empty.
- The den spot from where the throat-tube has started is called in Jalandhar, the head should slightly bend or, in other words, the backbone is not hundred per cent straight. By slightly bending the head jalandhar bundh, (Bundh means close), is done. The navel part is called Uddiyan or the centre of the abdominal part.

Practically speaking, during meditation, these actions take place automatically. It is therefore an intuitive pose.

By closing up the activities of these parts – the anus, the navel or abdomen and the throat den (Kanthakoop) the vital wind – Prana starts running into the central canal of the backbone. Meditation at the start has Satvik inclination – virtuous traits of human nature, compassion, love for seclusion, asexuality, etc. So long as the vital wind fails to have an access to this part of the backbone called schushmna, the meditator meditates not on God but on thoughts connected with rajas or tamas (or fair or bad elements of his characters respectively). This is the spiritual aspect of this kriya (Yoga actions). As for health, the following are the benefits.

- It destroys wind in the stomach.
- Stomach diseases vanish day-by-day.
- Pancreas is fuelled with an invisible energy so that meditators feel a buoyant spirit, but no appetite actually, although the body feels lightness.
- The pose has a direct hygienic bearing upon the spleen, liver and stomach. As a result, it reduces the complaints or cures the diseases connected with these parts.
- It brings down the temperature of the body, therefore, it is an anti-fever pose, but one should maintain it about 20-25 minutes minimum.
- At the start, this pose is done in the lotus part and the toes of the legs are caught by the two hands crosswise. The left hand is taken through the back and the left toes are held firmly, while the right hand is taken through the back and right toes are held firmly. The posture is also called badda padmasan or preparatory yogamudra.

Home Remedies

- Ordinary fever can be fought effectively by the following process.
- Basil leaf and stem (both) should be mixed with a quantity of black pepper and a reasonable quantity of water. Boil it for some time; strain it to make a decoction. Drink it once or twice a day.
- Success pose is also effective to bring down the temperature. Half an hour is the minimum time needed for the purpose.
- A combination of a reasonable quantity of water, one lemon, rock salt, and black pepper can be used to beat the rise of temperature.
- Fasting with boiled water only.

Liver Diseases

Diet during fever

A lot of barley boiled with sugar candy is said to be a best fever diet. During fever one should not eat anything after the sunset.

Garudasana (Bird Pose)

Garud means vulture. So, the pose is called Garudasana.

Procedure

- Stand erect.
- Overlap the back part of any leg (near the ankle and above) with the other one; while, the hands would overlap each other.
- The head should not now be erect but considerably bent forward. This bending is done for treating scrotum disease, Hernia, Hydrocele or Orchitis. In all these cases, the entire genitalia should be placed behind and between the thighs so that scrotum is comfortably but tightly pressed. The affected side should be given special attention. Fasting on boiled water only can combat the intensity of the attack. The diet must not be wind-producing.

Garudasana (Bird Pose)

Persons whose legs shiver on account of weakness will be benefited by this pose also.

Lotus Balance Pose

This is also called hill pose or mountain pose.

Speaking of Curing Diseases through Yoga

Procedure
- Sit preferably in the lotus pose as this pose is congenial to maintain the balance, if not possible, use ordinary pose which is a little inconvenient to balance the body.
- Now stand up on the knees.
- Raise your hands and join them and stay in this position for some time.

Lifted Lotus Pose

The lotus pose may be done in a variety of ways. In lifted lotus pose, sit in lotus pose and put your hands outside the thighs on the floor. Now lift your entire body with help of your hands which are firmly placed on the ground.

Lifted Lotus Pose

Devotion Pose

Sit in any of the following poses: success pose lotus half cow mouth goraksha pose, expansion of legs or ordinary pose.

You need a Mala (rosary) having 108 or 54 beads. The number 108 is sacred because in Yoga, Intuitive experiences, petals of different numbers, namely, 108, 1008, are prescribed in the stages of chakras. Hold on the mala in the right hand, and not left hand (for right hand is

Devotion Pose

Liver Diseases

used in sacred works namely worshipping, etc.) and not the left hand. As per yoga rules, the food is supposed to be served with the right hand only as far as is practicable. However, to count the beads, raise your right hand at the chest but do not touch the chest. A sacred spirit of devotion really would emanate from this mood and mode. It is a good pose for collecting the dispersed mind.

Lecture Pose or Sermon Pose

There are complaints of maya by some public spiritual instructors that their minds succumb to violent aggression of lower senses when they catch sight of beautiful damsels listening to their discourses in a devout spirit.

This pose is a grand physiological way to arrest the evil run of the lower senses. This pose is similar to half cow mouth pose. The only difference is that you sit with your thighs crossed. By performing Brahmacharya asana, Expansion of legs pose, Half Cow Mouth Pose, Pashchimotanasana and Lecture Pose the sexual glands stop secreting preparatory seminal fluid and hence the economy becomes free of any turbulence, irritation or excitement.

Benefits

- The pose arrests the flow of the sexual glands thereby making them dry so that although the mind, the bone of contention, is really difficult to be brought under control absolutely, the physiological distastefulness helps the doer to check the lower sense nuisance at least for the time being and the doer is saved from being deviated from the state.
- Keep changing the legs if one starts paining.

50. Ear Complaints

Karnapeerasana

Karna means 'ear', and *peerh*, 'stir, strain or torment'. The pose helps to maintain the health of the ears but it has other benefits too. First of all, it helps to reduce the flaccidity of the performer; secondly, it makes the backbone supple gradually; thirdly, important indeed – it is beneficial against lung diseases like bronchitis, asthma, cough, cold, etc.

Karnapeerasana

Procedure

- Lie down on the back stretching out the legs fully.
- Perform shoulder stand pose (Sarvangasana).
- Now take your feet behind the head slowly.
- Set the knees at the ears while the lower part of the legs should remain straight.
- The feet may also be stretched out parallel to the ground.
- Press the ears gently.
- Maintain the stay for some time.

Ear Complaints

Other Measures for Maintaining Good Health of the Ears

- The medicinal way of maintaining the health of the ears is to use a few drops of pure mustard oil mixed with a pinch of rock salt before taking bath every day.
- The wax in the ear should be cleaned every day in this way, and this will ensure that no infection occurs in the future. Karnapeerasana is also helpful in purifying the blood..

However temporary protective remedies against ill health of the ears are as follows:-

- If a foreign element (worm etc.) intrudes into the ear, the best way is to put some drops of tepid water mixed with a little salt. Water can also be substituted with mustard oil.
- Strained onion juice, slightly warmed in fire if put in the ear (three or four drops), will alleviate pain in the ear temporarily.
- Garlic juice to be mixed with a little hot mustard oil can destroy abscess or boil in the ear (Garlic juice is better than onion juice).
- The biggest toe should be smeared with mustard oil considerably. Navel and nostrils can also be smeared with mustard oil.
- Do not put anything sharp or pointed inside the ear.
- Eyes should be smeared in the same way to avoid inflammation, etc.

All these should be done every day before taking bath.

51. Breathing Exercises or Pranayama

For the purpose of maintaining health or curing diseases, the asanas that have been dealt with so far are enough. The asanas have been selected and prescribed on the basis of the reports obtained from the students, patients and the various researches done on them.

    A slight hint on the breathing exercises is being given to those who are willing to strengthen the spiritual aspect of their lives too. In fact, breathing exercises or Pranayama is a subject of a very finer perception. Respiration is only a manifestation of a gross form from a subtle bottom. Doctors can discover till it is connected with respiration which is but a manifestation. But in the subtle form there lies the mind which is not objective or material; it is apparently connected with the function of the senses, namely, respiratory organs. Thus, it is said that the mind becomes still when the pranas are still; and the lower self (the individual self connected with I-ness), being forgetful of its illness, copulates with the Self proper. This physiological affair takes place in the human economy through breathing exercises which our sages have invented through their Yogic insight. Thus, in every round of Pranayama, the question of retention of breathing arises and in each retention the aspirant comes closer to the Being at a snail's pace. In every retentive state, the mind is expected to taste the silence on the condition that the mind is sincerely sincere to acquire the Silence, but in most cases the aspirants' mind is not sincere as a result he enjoys sound health on account of a good variety of Yoga of asanas, pranayamas or in, other words, Yoga of health but from the spiritual point of view, he fails to attain the target (Being).

Breathing Exercises or Pranayana

Thus, the hindrance of the spiritual aspect of Yoga is told. As for health, let it be known to the patients that pranayama is a matter of a very subtle nature. Therefore, it requires the following rules and regulations to get the maximum benefit:

- The stomach should preferably be empty or one can take something light.
- The stomach should not be too windy. Pranayama is possible only when the wind is evacuated from the stomach.
- The doer should increase it very slowly and cautiously with the help of a Guru or Teacher. Self-styled teachership may cost the precious health.
- The doer must not indulge in excessive discharge of the vital fluid from the body.
- Try to take more of a liquid diet.
- Forceful increase of Pranayama may create heaviness of the head, i.e. headache.
- The yoga aspirant should talk very less as compared to non-aspirants.

The following types of Pranayama are enough, if continued for life, improving one's spiritual as well as physical state:

1. Inhale air with the right nostril if it is day (and not evening or night) exhale with the left nostril without retaining the breath. Start this process slowly and gradually do it as fast as you can. The faster it is done, better is the preparation for the retentive variety. Inhalation can also be done with both the nostrils and so the exhalation most rapidly. The result is same. In each inhalation, the stomach should be lifted up with force and in exhalation, it should be thrown down. Continue it many times.

2. Retentive Variety: Follow the formula 1:4:2 or, inhalation, retention and exhalation. Inhale and retain four times the time spent inhalation and, then, exhale in about half the time of retention.

Speaking of Curing Diseases through Yoga

These two varieties of Pranayamas are enough.

Pranayama is done in the lotus pose. Some sages advocated to do this in the Siddhasana too. No other poses are found prescribed by the sages. Pranayama doers should live mostly on liquid food, vegetable juice, milk, water, etc. Discharge of excessive semen incapacitates the door to retain air for a longer period of time.

- Consult an ayurvedic doctor

Other recommended asanas

- Shoulder stand
- Plough pose
- Fish pose
- Cow mouth (special attention) etc.

Diet

- Dates, abstention from eating starch food, sour, pungent, chilli, etc. Vegetable oil, fried food, ice cream are prohibited. Drink at least five litres of boiled water daily. In winter and rains, warm water should be taken. Bathe in hot water mixed with salt (any salt) in winter.

- Protect constipation by using Triphala. Garlic, ginger, honey etc. should be used a little more.

- The most efficacious way to fighting respiratory diseases is to meditate. Meditate on God, power, nature, energy, beautiful natural scenery or the self. To meditate deeply amounts to arresting respiration to a great extent. Meditate or do Japa for a long time in any pose.

- Deep meditation reduces respiratory complaints in a natural way without any medicine on the condition that yogic diet is observed nicely. Doctors are astonished to see the effects of meditation in a human body. Both Japa and meditation should be done for a long period of time – three hours non-stop.

Breathing Exercises or Pranayana

- Fasting is another greatest way to hold the irregular run of breathing in check in a most natural way. Fast once in ten days or, fast on the eleventh day of both the full moon and the new moon.
- Retentive variety of Pranayama is most useful. One should practise in consultation with a teacher to fight disease. Each asana should be done for a period of time to effect the complaints. Each asana has a staying position in which respiration is automatically held up – a fact which is highly useful for the body as well as the mind.
- Pranayama should be done for more than half an hour. Homoeopathic remedies are good in many cases if the doctor is good.

52. Dental Health

Ayurveda has a number of effective remedies for maintaining a good dental health. Some of them are given below:
- Stop eating meat.
- Don't eat sticky edibles.
- Don't eat something too hot or too cold.
- Brush your teeth with an ayurvedic medicine.
- Brushing with a Margo branch is really helpful.
- Don't try to break something with your teeth very hard with full force.
- Gargling with alum water every day is best for the gums. One fifth of one teaspoon of crushed alum with one glass of water after eating a meal is helpful.
- A mixture of turmeric and rock salt to be mixed with a quantity of mustard oil relieves toothache.
- A little mustard oil, three teaspoons of rock salt or common salt, a pinch of camphor, a pinch of clove dust or crushed clove and half a teaspoon of turmeric all mixed should be smeared on the teeth.
- Brushing the teeth is injurious or hazardous to gum especially to sufferers. Ayurvedic doctors advise to press the gums firmly when one passes stool. They opine it is healthy for the teeth. Its anatomical or biological reason is yet to be known. The reason is esoteric but it works.

Dental Health

- Spinach and carrot juice are said to be very much useful for teeth.
- The bark of a Jambul (Indian fruit) tree crushed and mixed with water is highly beneficial for gums and teeth.

Indigestion, constipation, gastritis, etc. are congenial to pave way for dental problems triphala churan should be consumed twice a day morning and at night before going to bed.

For Healthy Eyes

1. High power electric bulbs are injurious to eyes. Mercury bulbs are not bad.
2. Eyes should be (sprinkled with water for about some minutes) immediately after snacks, meals and sleep.
3. Fish is a useful food for eyes. It increases the eye sight and retards the ill health of eyes.
4. Oyster and snails are said to be beneficial to eyes.
5. Eye exercise especially while performing the fish pose is beneficial.
6. To look at the Sun for a time with eyes closed is useful.
7. Goggles, sunglasses are not good for eyes.
8. To maintain the regularity of circulation of blood, the eyes should be fomented with both hot (tepid) and cold water alternatively.
9. Collyrium is said to be effective.
10. Mustard oil is used to light a lamp. Collyrium is, thus, prepared from the black flame and held in a metal sheet or in a tree leaf and then used with fingers to smear the borders of both lids of an eye. Mothers in India use it for their infants. Some adult also use it.
11. Almond is a very useful eye sight.

Speaking of Curing Diseases through Yoga

12. Soya, mint, radish, carrot, grapes, pomegranate, cucumber, pineapple, fig, ginger, watermelon, melon, bitter gourd, Jambul, tomatoes, mango, jack fruit, coconut, sweet lime, turmeric, fenugreek, spinach, almond, cashew, lemon, honey, banana, onion, garlic, basil, apple, etc. are good for eyes.

53. Liberation or Salvation

Reverential prostration unto the sweet Lotus Feet of the sages of the yore!

The laity has a trillion day dreams. He is absorbed in brown study* round the clock. Out of a trillion dreams, hardly one is successful, because none of his dreams has its connection with the Absolute Being. To materialise a thought, the thinker should think from the state which is beyond sensorial i.e. which is supra sensorial. This being an impossibility for the laity on the ground of so many factors, namely especially, contaminated mind, in the first instance, he goes on building castles in the air, runs after a mirage of happiness from this worldly life but of no avail. He takes to birth with another castle in the air. This is what is called Samsar (world). But the ideas that emanate from the Unmanifest Being with whom the Yogi makes a wireless contact with the help of his immaculate heart, start materializing instantly.

How to cross this ocean of this vast sensory world the Yogi harps on the same string time and again, what asanas are applicable to make the naris more transparent, the Yogi thinks with a pensive mood, but definitely, in the name of God. Thus, the asanas, as stated in the educative and informative Forewords have come down from heaven to this earth of ours. The Yogi lives in a paradise of Bliss when he enjoys the serenity as he dives deep at the bottom of the Pacific.

Kandapeerasana, Liberation Pose or Moksha Asana is a manufacture of such a pious thinking and storehouse of Bliss enjoyed by the revered sages.

---

*day dreaming or building castles in the air

Speaking of Curing Diseases through Yoga

Transcendence, truly speaking, is a hard nut to crack for, body consciousness is not to be gone away so long as there is a slightest feeling of body or slightest particle of desire lying dormant in the human mind. *Raso Opi Asya Parang DrishtwaNivartat A* – unless Transcendence is achieved, nescient love for worldliness – my wife, my child, my friend, my name, my fame, my bank balance, my lover, my designation and the like cacophonous blabs are not to be disappeared from the mind; Peace, therefore, is a far cry. But Yoga is the way – the sages direct. Well! Yoga is the way – which Yoga calls for Transcendence, surely it is the burning question. The answer to such an inquisitiveness is the Asana under discussion.

The range of actions for acquisition of Yoga – the Holy Communion is from the anus to the crown, simply speaking. Even as a bamboo tree has knots one after another, the human physiology has some states of Yoga that start from the anus to the crown. Other manifestations in different parts of the body in different forms or ways – shaking, jerking etc. takes place outwardly when the inner system is overhauled, ransacked or rummaged through Yoga Asanas and Kriyas. And among the most powerful ransacking processes, Kandapeerasana ranks highest because, as it has been stated in the Shakti Chalani Moodra, the navel part from where the countless, Yogis have enumerated the number 72,000, Naris have energized the entire human economy from the crown or every nook and corner of the body, is the most important part of a human being. The benedictions of such a beautiful physical posture are also excellent and numerous, because the incidence of this pose of the human anatomy is marvelous. A few of them only are being enumerated here under keeping an eye to the volume of the book:

1) The Pran Vayu (vital force) is seized, arrested and, then brought to the Sushumna – a fact which is responsible for stilling the mind and, therefore, controlling the thought vibrations that run wild to kill the Serene state of the meditator.

Liberation or Salvation

2) The proof of the run of the vital force, to the Sushumna is that, among other symptoms, the aspirant feels as if a coin is set to the central part of his brows. But that should be sustained by the doer with all sincerity and earnestness or else, the state would disappear like camphor as intuitive knowledge reveals.

3) Diseases related to liver, spleen, anus, rectum intestines- large and small, duodenum, displacement of arteries and veins, displacement of navel, pancreas – in a word, the entire region is effected, not slightly but severely and powerfully.

4) The Evil Spirit who is responsible for creating knee-joint pains suffered by aspirants of old age especially, is killed or, in other words, knee-joint pains are destroyed at its grass roots if, definitely, dietetic rules are followed. This pose shall guard knee-joint pains, although it is unwise to follow top class Yogasanas while disobeying the dietetic rules. After all, Nature has its role to play more or less according to the way She is treated.

5) Patients suffering from dizziness, vertigo, various kinds of headaches, insomnia, restlessness of mind, fidgety legs, forgetfulness, lack of spiritual IQ, etc. can derive maximum benefit out of this grand posture.

6) Kandpeerasana or Liberation Pose empowers the mind to sort out the Real from the unreal, i.e. haphazard thought vibrations of mind. The intellect being purged of unnecessaries, the enjoyer reaches the Destination direct without any stoppage- although it happens occasionally in the beginning days of practice. No literary talent is enough to express this beautitude in words. The performer is overwhelmed with the Self, to say the least.

Even as ants are contended with a few grains of sugar unlike an elephant that needs at least one quintal to fill only a part of hunger, so a Yogi of Highest aspiration requires something special to reach the Unlimited and is not, therefore satisfied with a few primary states of God consciousness.

The central part of the eye brows – as the *Gita* imparts "*Bhruboremadh A Pranam Abeshya Samyak*" is a sure indication of nearness to the Self, as the Unlimited starts from the central part of the crown- the Vast Azure of Fullness of Nothingness. The *Gita* which has explained Yoga events in many chapters in many different ways directly and indirectly, is a storehouse of wisdom. The Gita declares, "any aspirant can remember His name in his death bed, while the vital force reaches through the central part of the brows, attains the Self or Almighty God."

Body consciousness is bound to be disturbing the mind so long as the aspirant's vital force (prana) runs not above the navel; the lesser is the thought, the higher, therefore, is the position of the Prana in the body. Number of thoughts is in proportion to the height of the Pranavayu. Thoughts start reducing its number and upgrading its quality (i.e. transformed into piety) as it Ascends into the Heaven, to explain poetically. This is a great secret of Yoga events but hushed up by the Yogis for, the laity would underestimate the precious events that come across by the Yogis.

This asana is a guarantor of a large number of asanas. In addition to subtle functioning of this pose in the economy, this pose is a great remedy against psychic diseases, if diet is observed properly.

To make this coveted posture a grand success, the followings may be called the preparatory attempts;

- Expansion of legs (important)
- Hasta Padasana (hand touch feet)
- Sitting standing (till it starts paining unbearably) another most important.
- Paschimottanasana (also called forward Bending pose)
- Bhunmanasana (touch the floor with your chin while maintaining the expansion of legs)

Liberation or Salvation

- Toe kissing while standing.

To venture such an extraordinary or, almost supernatural asana, the aspirant should drink two cups of milk mixed with two spoonfuls of turmeric powder on an empty stomach for several days and, follow the same dose after an interval of some days. The remedy helps to supple the bone hardened by unwanted filthy products. Night food should be less and should be dominated more by liquid food than by stuffy food.

Liberation Pose

Procedure

- Sit against a wall,
- Fold any of your legs directing it towards your chest gently, slowly but with a strong determination,
- Do the same process with the other leg also.
- Now, take the help of the wall and pull both the legs towards the chest. You are sure to fall down many times. Be prepared for that.
- After doing this for several days, stop for few days and start again. You may experience a rise in your body temperature. When the pose is brought under control successfully, follow tribundh, i.e. maintain closure of anus, navel part and throat. Bend forward five degrees or slightly. Expand your chest as in the picture. Close your eyes as shown in the photo. Maintain the stay.
- Use homoeopathic remedy for pain – three or four drops of Arnica 30 to be put on the tongue in the morning on an empty stomach. Water your mouth with hot water before taking the medicine. Do not eat, drink or smoke within at least half an hour of taking the medicine. Use this remedy every day for several days.

Benefits

Shakti Chalani Moodra may be done before the liberation pose if the pose is treated as a pose of meditation. If not, the moodra may be done after the pose. This Liberation pose, Mokshasana or Kandapeerasaana should not be treated as a pose for meditation, but the scriptures advise to follow this pose for them who want to maintain yogic health that paves the way for the Higher States of Consciousness. It is a grandest means to enter the kingdom of meditation on account of its vital role in opening up the subtlest invisible canals of the economy. If the channel of knowledge- Saraswati Nari or Sushumna, as it has been respectfully termed by the sages by so many names, is transparent, the mind which is the bone of contention wandering here and there only Godly or pious thought-vibrations dominate. If the Nari is not neat and clean, no one can enter kingdom of transcendence, whatsoever may be the aspirant's profile in respect of name, fame, wealth, appearance, discipleship- nothing counts in the kingdom of Righteousness. Nepotism has no role to play in the kingdom of God. The aspirant should feel the intuitive events personally with his own flesh and blood without being carried away by lofty talks.

True, intuitive knowledge is the personal milestone of one's destination even if he is not liberated. What is the use of running after Gurus if one is not heartily disciplined or sincere? Personal experience is a produce of one's own sincerity.

Be Not a Braggart

"I am a football champion. How dare you advise me to be cautious"? vaunted one poor beginner. And lo! As he tried to fold his legs with a drastic helter skelter, he broke his leg and the author had to hospitalise the braggart. It is, therefore, better to take the help of a qualified teacher.

May God Bestow His Blessings on us all according to our Karma.

Om Peace!

Liberation or Salvation

Easiest Meditation Posture

Although utmost attempts have been made in this book to pave the way for the aspirants to follow several varieties of postures recommended for meditation, one more system as entitled above can be introduced. Like some postures that have been discovered, tested and verified by the author himself, this is another decipherment. See to it yourself by following the rules laid down hereunder.

This pose as the title suggests, is convenient to those who cannot fold their legs to the extent of the lotus pose or who cannot set their feet to the nook of the legs and thighs.

Procedure

- First and foremost, sit perfectly erect.
- Stretch out your legs and set one foot on the other.
- Bend your head slightly forward making an angle of a few degrees with your shoulder so as to make the tribundh effective.
- The two knees must lie flat on the ground. It will happen by dint of repeated practices only, so don't bother about it.
- Set your hands on the knees respectively, fingers can be posed as shown.
- Close your eyes.
- Forget not to maintain the mool bundh – the most important factor of inner world accession.
- While maintaining the mool bundh – one may easily concentrate on the body points as laid down in the mind concentration topic.
- Remember His or Deity's divine countenance by doing so you will only help yourself to enjoy the real ecstatic state of meditation or if meditation is a tough nut to crack for you, just count the beads of a rosary, of course with a sincere piety.

Speaking of Curing Diseases through Yoga

- Chest should be expanded, the backbone must not be curved.
- Stay around half an hour on an average with your eyes closed.

Meditation when the aspirant becomes a veteran practitioner is an automatic process as per the laws of Nature. Some patients reported that it cured their age-old problem of headache, sleeplessness, etc.

Some report that it is an alternative system of Vipassana system of meditation as named and introduced by Shri S.N. Goenka.

54. Yogasanas Further Discussed

Among the mudras that have a most powerful impact on the human physiology for the sole purpose of propitiating the Mother Kundalini - after shakti chalani mudra, khechari mudra is the most important.

This mudra is performed before the liberation pose generally. Shakti chalani mudra paves the way for cleansing the naris - the subtle invisible energy channels or canals which have spread their tentacles all over the system of the human economy. The kand situated a little below the navel is stirred by the kriya so much so that the practitioner starts sweating.

As the Sun is energised by the Omnipotent and the Sun God has dispersed His blessings to the universe in all directions but with an unequal proportion even slightest, the nanipur chakra, a little below the navel, is kneaded.

Heavy asanas already done by the aspirant and the stomach being empty and, the doer's celibacy being highly appreciable, he then, feels a strong mood of introversion incapacitating him to glide on this material world. His eyes are shut down like a mimosa leaf automatically, and the real joy of Yoga starts working little by little well before he starts doing Pranayama which will again, deepen the serenity inexpressible.

Caution

A large number of practitioners feel excitement of the lower senses whether male or female. Most successful weapon to fight the situation is to have a glass of cold water. For male aspirants, some may even have an erection. Another way to fight the situation is to sit in the half cow mouth pose for a period of time. These remedies are applicable to both male and female.

Vastrika Pranayama

Vastrika Pranayama in which nostrils are blown at one and the same time with a heavy sound, are done automatically.

Shakti Chalani Mudra

Procedure

- Sit down
- Fold your legs and press the navel with your heels.
- Exhale and inhale as fast as you can, but in the beginning go slowly.
- Go on accomplishing the yogic kriya till you start sweating.
- Have rest, if exhausted.
- Try it again

Shakti Chalani Mudra

If tired follow the dead pose. Mouth, however, should be kept closed during the kriya. To inhale with mouth open is injurious to health. Forceful respiration may create headache or heaviness in the head. If it does happen, stop the kriya and take rest for some days and, then, do it again. You may need more vigorous asanas – each asana for a longer period of time to cleanse the naris of the impurities.

Yogasanas Further Discussed

Camel posture is helpful in treating the following problems:
- Navel displacement
- Malfunctioning of backbone
- Intestinal dislodgement of arteries and veins, etc.
- Constipation
- Pot belly
- Largeness of posterior
- Diabetes
- Dyspepsia
- Chest pain
- Angina pectoris
- Neck ache
- Spondilitis

Caution

Patients of hernia and testicle diseases should watch their problems and consult a physician.

- As soon as a female conceives, practise of yogic asana should be stopped completely.
- Females should abstain from performing asanas during menstruation as in some cases it may lead to heavy bleeding.
- To make a rapid development in Yoga (of asanas), living on liquid foods as much as possible is the best way.
- Practising asanas at dawn is more impressive. During the practise of asanas, closure of the three parts of the practitioner, namely anus, mouth and eyes should be maintained to derive maximum results.
- Hot drinks, hot water, cigarettes, tobacco, etc. should never be taken immediately after yoga as the economy is already

Speaking of Curing Diseases through Yoga

heated up. Water, fruit, curd, rice, lemon juice, orange juice, etc. however, are allowed.
- Take a bath hot or cold according to the climate. A bath before Yoga is congenial.
- Regular practitioners should not perform surya namaskar twice a day; it would be like overexerting yourself. Irrespective of any complaints, the spiritualists should follow the following directions.

One hour programme
1. Close your eyes, sit erect, and think positive for some minutes.
2. Maintain the closure of eyes and perform headstand and rest pose.
3. Tone up your body from head to foot.
4. Rolling (several times on right and left).
5. Cycling (fast as you can) for some minutes.
6. Camel pose
7. Pashchimottan pose
8. Veepareet karani mudra
9. Shoulder stand pose
10. Plough pose
11. Fish pose
12. Wheel pose
13. Peacock pose
14. Cow mouth
15. Matsyendra pose
16. Yoga mudra
17. Nari shodhasana

Yogasanas Further Discussed

18. Tree pose
19. Scorpion pose
20. Mahamudra
21. Kanda Peerasan
22. Sheersasana
23. Rest pose
24. Gorakshasana

Eyes should not be opened as much as possible. Accomplish some nauli actions on an empty stomach. Meditate or rest with eyes closed.

Half an hour programme for busy people:

1. Sun salutation
2. Squatting
3. Wheel pose
4. Paschimottan pose
5. Half Matsyendra pose (twisting of spinal cord)
6. Rest pose
7. Navel exercise
8. Meditation

55. Nauli

Nauli

Procedure

- Lie down on your back.
- Have rest for some seconds.
- Lift up your entire stomach while inhaling and throw the entire stomach down to the navel with a gasping sound.

Sukhasana or the Ordinary Pose

Ordinary Pose: For various reasons, some adopt this posture which is very simple, but if the doer is sincerely earnest, the pose is as good as other poses because sincerity of the purpose is the burning question. However, the back should not be bent and mool bandh in this pose is advised for the purpose of having an access to innerness.

Psychological Benefits: If this asana is practised regularly along with an intake of balanced diet the doer can get rid of all the tension, stress and strain.

Nauli in the expansion of legs pose

56. Some other Problems

Cholera

A germ-borne disease with fever, loose motion, cramps, etc. Yogic kriyas, fasting with boiled water. Fast with liquid foods only.

Anaemia

Remedies

Eat a lot of green vegetable juice (as much as can be digested). Eat red beat a lot. Eat it in vegetables including the foliage which is more useful and helps in formation of blood. Chew your food properly.

Sunsalutations, sitting standing, peacock pose, matsyendrasana, etc. are most important. Follow yoga daily.

Apoplexy

Remedies

Unwanted run of blood in the head, unusual circulation of blood. Imbalance of wind in the body is another great cause.

- Regular practice of Yoga with strict dietetic rules. Head stand, peacock pose, sun salutations, matsyendra pose and kandpeerasana (liberation pose).
- Keep your stomach absolutely unconstipated (use Triphala- an Ayurvedic preparation twice a day). Use Ayurvedic hair oil. Feed mostly on liquid food (so, physical work should not be much).

- Meditate thrice a day.
- Guard against formation of wind in the stomach.
- Intake of pungent foods and drinks is prohibited.

Angina Pectoris (Pain in the chest)

Remedies

Fish pose, sun salutations, salt fomentation, shoulder stand pose, plough pose, tree pose, etc. Eat more grapes.

Aneurism

Remedies

Dilation of an artery transformed into a tumor, an infection or too much smoking, etc.

- Regular practice of Yoga with dietetic rules,
- Fasting with boiled water once a week,
- Starch food should be avoided.

Asthma

Remedies

- Medical condition which makes breathing difficult
- Take all preventive measures for not catching cold.
- A combination of black pepper, ginger, garlic juice and honey works in an acute state.
- Starch food is highly uncongenial.
- Sun salutation calls for a special attention.
- Protect acute condition with fasting with boiled water.
- Follow walking, breathing – the process-inhale for two steps, retain for eight steps and exhale in four steps or, breathe in for a time while walking, retain for some steps and then release. It may improve an acute condition.

Some other Problems

Aphonia (Loss of voice)

Remedies

- Ayurvedic and Homoeopathic remedies work. Maintain dead silence or taciturnity.
- Garlic, ginger, honey and black pepper are useful.
- Gargle with ginger-mixed hot water.
- Stop eating starch food.

Amblyopia (Defective vision)

Remedies

- *Tratak-* Gaze at an object of your choice for a time till your eyes start watering. Fish pose with eye exercise should work. Fresh fish is highly beneficial for eyes.
- Cashew nuts, etc. are good for eyes.
- Tobacco, alcohol and lead poison should be avoided.

Adenoids (A soft, velvety mass in the nostrils)

Remedies

- Abstain from starch food,
- Use thread-wash (Sutra Neti) to protect the complaint in future.
- Practise Vastrika every day.
- Regular practice of Yoga can prevent this complaint.
- Fasting with water may relieve the intensity of the disease.

Appendicitis (Inflammation of appendix)

Remedies

- Highly spiced non-vegetarian food or wrong eating habits is a cause.

- Keep your stomach clean, i.e. unconstipated.
- Eat mostly liquids.
- No pungent food and drink should be taken.
- Stomach should be kept cooled.
- In acute conditions, a glass of water with about 20 grams of sugar candy may relieve the pain to some extent.

Albuminuria

Remedies

- Caused by albuminous diet, e.g. eggs, etc. or by excessive intake of cold water. The disease is connected with kidney, urine, etc.
- Yogic diet.
- Matsyendrasana (most important), peacock pose and intake of boiled water – liberation pose (kandapeerasana).

Acromegaly (Excessive secretion of foreign matter from the brain leading to enlargement of bones in the head)

Remedies

- Yogic asanas will not help in an acute condition.

Hepatitis (Inflammation, irritation or burning sensation of the liver)

Remedies

- Caused mostly by injurious pungent diet, wine or pungent spices.
- Yogic asanas can help only little unless unhygienic diet is given up. After taking to any system of medicine, the patient should follow stomach and liver-related poses.

Some other Problems

Papaya, radish, fruit or vegetable juice is good. Edibles fried in oil are not at all congenial. Raw fruit juice or vegetable juice is a good diet.

Herpes (A kind of skin disease connected with anus)

Remedies

- Follow skin disease, yoga exercises and instructions. Go through the Fistula topics.

Influenza (A rise in body temperature with headache, coryza, etc. Doctors are of the opinion that it is an epidemic disease sometimes)

Remedies

- Siddhasana (adept pose) for a period of about an hour without break helps to check the problem.
- Fasting with success pose works more. Black tea with lemon several times a day works a lot.
- Barley is good for influenza or fever.

Convulsions (Abnormal gesticulations, movement of limbs and\or eyes)

Remedies

- Chronic constipation is said to be the root cause.
- Stomach wash once a week, live on plain food, give up smoking, alcohol, tobacco, etc.
- Sprinkling of water on the face is the best way.
- Use hot and cold water alternately in a running condition, loosen the clothes and lie down in a dead pose.
- Meditate several times a day. Eat at a fixed time.

- Eating at night food should either be avoided or should be substituted by a liquid food.

Irritation (stung by insects, worms etc)

Remedies

- Ripe tamarind works, its rind or fibre should be thrown away but the fruit (one fruit is enough) should be used. Half of the fruit should be eaten up while the other half should be set to the spot and bandaged with a mop or polythene.
- Avoid drinking water or liquid within two hours of treatment. Onion juice if applied to the spot also works. Sour fruit juice helps to cool down the irritation in a short time.
- An ointment of powdered black pepper and pure honey if applied to the spot is said to work faster than the above remedy. Simultaneously, the following homoeopathic remedy should work with a double effect.
- Homoeopathic remedy against scorpion bite – Arsenicum Alb- 30 or, Arsenicum Alb- 200 is useful. (Dose Just two or three drops in an acute state). Nothing should be eaten or drunk within a few hours.
- Treatment with tamarind also works for a scorpion bite but not for all.

Morbus (Hip joint disease)

Remedies

- Bow pose, wheel pose, Pashchimootanasana, nari shodhanasan, locust pose, bhunmanasana and sun salutations, etc. call for a special attention.
- Avoid having food at night. Fast once in a week, avoid starch food absolutely. The usage of garlic, honey, black

pepper should be a little more keeping an eye to excessive usage.
- Avoid sour food curd.

Nephritis (Inflammation of the kidneys)

Remedies

- Warm clothing, warm drinks and absolutely bland food and drink all help to lessen the intensity of the complaint.
- Among the poses matsyendrasana, veepareet karani mudra, peacock, bow pose, camel pose, gorakhasana, etc. are of special attention.
- Drink four litres of boiled water a day.
- Meat is injurious.
- The Matsyendrasana should be done for a period of time- say ten minutes for each leg.

Paralysis (Inability to move a part or some parts of the body, caused by cold, sitting in a fixed place or by poisoning)

Remedies

- Fasting with water accompanied with a moderate variety of yoga will improve the condition.
- Among the asana – toning, rolling, cycling, camel pase, sun salutation, peacock pose, sitting standing, matsyendrasana, narishodhanasana, etc. are of special importance. Regular practise will improve the condition gradually however, medication should not be stopped.
- Guard against constipation.
- Avoid sour foods, rice, lentils and, curd.
- Headstand should be done for a longer period of time.

Palpitation of Heart (Throbbing of heart at an abnormal rate, caused by emotions, wrong eating habits, arthritis or uneven circulation of blood)

- See heart disease.
- Sweating sun salutation, plough pose, pashchimathan pose, tree pose, scorpion pose etc. are very important. The patient, in an acute condition, may follow dead pose and see the result. It is reported that it works. A strong guard against constipation should be maintained.

Phlebitis (Inflammation of some parts of the body, namely, arteries, veins, tip of the fingers of both hands and legs)

Remedies

- Hot fomentation is comfortable in acute cases.
- The food should not be irritating, i.e. pungent.
- Bland food is good for the purpose.
- Curd may be eaten as a dessert.

Pyrosis (Eructations from the mouth generally caused by stomach malfunctioning)

Remedies

- The complaint leads to halitosis (offensive breathing). Warm water, if drunk in an acute condition helps for the time being in an acute condition.
- Stomach wash is a must at least once in one week.
- Regular yoga with a special attention to Sunsalutations and sitting standing, peacock pose, scorpion pose, matsyendrasana, half tortoise pose, etc. are of special importance.

Some other Problems

- Improve liver condition with proper food and regular practice of yoga.

Prurituani (Itching of anus)

Remedies

- Go through the system mentioned in the fistula topic. Guard against constipation and follow yoga twice a day.
- In an acute condition, an ointment made from coconut oil mixed, onion juice helps when applied at the anus.

Prolapsusani (Falling of the bowel)

Remedies

- Stop eating stuffy food as much as possible.
- Live mostly on liquid food. Practise yoga twice a day.
- Special attention should be given to veepareet karani mudra, Pashchimootanasana pose, headstand, etc.
- Camel pose is another good pose for the purpose.

Peritonitis (Intestine disease – irritation or inflammation of abdominal cavity membrane)

Remedies

- Fasting.
- Nauli and regular practices of asanas twice a day.
- Stomach wash is a must.
- Bland food is advisable.
- Sugar candy is more useful than sugar. The cooking oil should be coconut oil instead of any other.
- A glass of sugar candy mixed with water works in an acute condition. One tamarind or one big onion also works in a running condition.

- Rice gruel if eaten also works in an acute condition.

Syncope (Fainting fit, swooning)

Remedies

- It is mostly hereditary and can also caused due to wrong eating habits.
- Maintain fasting with either boiled water or with juices of fruits or vegetables.
- Avoid eating food at night.
- Fruit or vegetable juices should be mixed with a quantity of ginger juice or black pepper to avoid formation of wind in the stomach. Practise yoga thrice a day.
- Meditate three to four times a day.
- Avoid negative society and negative people. Avoid emotional disturbances.

Sea sickness (Vertigo, retching, headache and vomiting while travelling by sea)

Remedies

- Fasting with vegetable or fruit juice is very much useful, along with it, Yoga should be done twice a day.
- Matsyendrasana, headstand, wheel pose, scorpion pose are of special importance.
- Guard against constipation.
- Homoeopathic medicines work.
- Maintain headstand pose for a longer period of time.

Sycosis

(It is a germ disease. Itching of beard. It is transmissible to others because it is highly contagious).

Remedies
- Yogic asanas can prevent recurrence but cannot be of any helps in an acute state.
- The razor used by one should be kept in a boiling water for some minutes and then again washed with an antiseptic water.

Whitlow (Swelling, inflammation, pain, etc. of the finger, head or toes of the legs)

Remedies
- It may be caused by a wrong cut of nails or sometimes by infections too.
- Yoga of asanas has almost nothing to do with the acute condition, however, starch food and night food should be avoided in an acute condition.
- Hot fomentation works in a running condition.

Erythema (Inflammation of the skin)

It is a minor variety of skin disease. Therefore, skin disease topic should be followed.

Remedies

(The findings have been gained after a research on the student and patients for a period of time. The author himself is not a doctor but a Yoga practitioner and the asanas and the dietatic rules given in the book to prevent or cure many complicative diseases is mainly on the basis of experimental verification).

Allergy of Cold

The body starts reacting on account of a slightest provocation of cold. The economy is affected by a slightest cold so much so that there are severe bouts of sneezing, running nose, closure of nasal passages (either one nostril or both − a fact incapacitating the patient to breathe. Respiration is held up absolutely so that the patient is afraid of dying from suffocation, although he does not die but undergoes to face the music of his Karma). Until the repercussion of Karma is over, all his attempts end in smoke, except, apparently, a temporary relief with medicines. One nostril being blocked, the victim has to use the other. Inflammation or itching of eyes is also experienced severely.

Causes

Change of climate or lack of vitamin C, old Doctors opine, is the root cause. The virus finds an entry into the body lacking the said vitamin through a cold state of the body. Damp air, unventilated accommodations and even nearness to old books as per health magazines are said to be the predisposing causes.

Yogic Remedy

- "It takes a week if medicine is taken to or it takes seven days, if not taken to..." it is so said humorously. Yoga practitioners can avert the problem if regularity is maintained and sufficient care and caution is taken especially in regard to food and drink, the effect of which should not create cold in the stomach.

- Ice, curd, green onion, most of the lentils, cold water both for drinking and bathing should be stopped.

- As for asanas, sun salutations, peacock pose, yogmudra and especially hare pose are important.

- Vastrika pranayama can help a lot to guard against worsening the condition. Some patients may fail to perform in an acute condition on account of lack of patience.

Other Measures and Diet

- Bathe in a hot water or take no bath at all if there is no headache. Keep the crown of the head warm therefore, use a winter cap.

Some other Problems

- Do not catch cold in any way.
- Gram, honey, ginger, garlic, lentil (only the pink colour variety is advisable), black tea with ginger juice and honey, etc.
- Water compress could be useful for inflammation of eyes.
- For the closure of nostrils, Saradindu oil- an ayurvedic preparation, is of sufficient help. But starch food, potato, spinach, mustard oil, red chilli are disease aggravating food. Milk and milk products are considered to intensify the complaint.
- However, even in a severe attack the following remedy has been proved to be efficacious.
- Take about half a teaspoon of black pepper, grind it nicely; boil two cups of water; put 15 or 20 pieces of fresh basil leaves or if not available, three teaspoons of dry basil seeds should be mixed with about two cups of water and boiled till one cup of the mixture remains as the residue. Thus, the mixture of black pepper, basil leaves or seeds and a pinch of sugar, if taken in an acute condition will remedy the complaint in no time beyond expectation. Caution – Do not eat or drink anything within half an hour.
- In an acute condition, black pepper, dry ginger and Ajwain (Hindi name) also works for arresting sneezing a lot. This dose may be taken after every half an hour or less according to the intensity of attack.

Impaired Digestion

Remedies

- Mince ginger nicely, put it in lemon juice and add a very little quantity of rock salt. Eat the pieces of ginger– six or seven pieces each time. This will help in digestion. In fact, for a regular Yoga practitioner, this complaint is out of his dictionary.

- Collect some bark of a walnut tree. Crush and add water, boil and then, strain it. Drink on an empty stomach. This destroys worms.

Intestinal Worms

Remedies

- Green coconut is reported to kill intestinal worms. Homoeopathic remedy 'wormplex'– also works nicely in empty stomach. After having wormplex, it is better not to eat, drink anything or smoke at least for half an hour.
- Several leaves of Neem (margo), if chewed on an empty stomach for some days arrest the production of worms. Cashew, however, is a worm – destroying fruit. Make a decoction which should be used on an empty stomach. It is said that it destroys worms. Rock salt mixed with mint juice or mint leaves is useful in killing intestinal worms.

Ayurvedic Remedies

Chirata and kootki – half a teaspoonful of each, should be mixed in two cups of water. Boil till half a tea cup remains. Strain and drink on an empty stomach. Drink several days at a stretch. This is a good remedy against intestinal worms. Homoeopathic remedies can also be used simultaneously. Homoeopathic and ayurvedic medicines work without any side effects.

Toilet Motion Asana

Although a little has been discussed in regard to the remedial postures connected with constipation, yet a new posture has been invented in order to fight unruly constipation responsible for manufacturing a number of highly complicated diseases that call for even surgical operations that may cost your happiness, peace and valuable financial resources.

This pose is done immediately after skipping for about one hundred times. Before skipping, it is better to drink about three

Some other Problems

glasses of tepid water mixed with salt lemon honey and rock salt but, black salt is preferable. Next to skipping, the patient may take to rolling many times both right and left. Rolling and skipping may be done alternately and vice versa according to the response available to the patients. The toilet motion pose may now be followed. The process is very easy indeed, but its effects are remarkable. The effect varies according to the intensity of the complaint.

Toilet Motion Asana

Procedure

- Have two or more glasses of water.
- Stand erect and inhale as much as possible,
- Bend forward by placing your hands on the knees,
- Retain the breath as much as you can,
- Come back to the former position when it is no more possible to retain the breath,
- Again inhale and bend forward and retain while the body is bent;
- Exhale while coming back to the former position.

Speaking repeatedly, a lot of green vegetables, either cooked or raw, are a guaranteed remedy against constipation. The patient should also undergo stomach wash at least once in ten days. The vegetables should especially be leafy and fibrous.

Note:- When the body rests on bending forward with hands on the respective knees, the head should not be bent but raised to the sky as much as possible. The legs should stand astride with a gap of about two feet. The asana stands sometimes ineffective if the head is not raised to the sky. The entire labour may fall flat. Inhalation should be started while standing and, then, the body, bent. Nauli of various processes is a greatest weapon to fight constipation.

■■■